Congressional Research Service
Informing the legislative debate since 1914

China and Proliferation of Weapons of Mass Destruction and Missiles: Policy Issues

Shirley A. Kan

Specialist in Asian Security Affairs

January 3, 2014

Congressional Research Service

7-5700

www.crs.gov

RL31555

I0417072

Summary

Congress has long been concerned about whether U.S. policy advances the national interest in reducing the role of the People's Republic of China (PRC) in the proliferation of weapons of mass destruction (WMD) and missiles that could deliver them. Recipients of China's technology reportedly included Pakistan, North Korea, and Iran. This CRS Report, updated as warranted, discusses the security problem of China's role in weapons proliferation and issues related to the U.S. policy response since the mid-1990s. China has taken some steps to mollify U.S. and other foreign concerns about its role in weapons proliferation. Nonetheless, supplies from China have aggravated trends that result in ambiguous technical aid, more indigenous capabilities, longer-range missiles, and secondary (retransferred) proliferation. Unclassified intelligence reports told Congress that China was a "key supplier" of technology, particularly with PRC entities providing nuclear and missile-related technology to Pakistan and missile-related technology to Iran.

Policy approaches in seeking PRC cooperation have concerned summits, sanctions, and satellite exports. PRC proliferation activities have continued to raise questions about China's commitment to nonproliferation and the need for U.S. sanctions. The United States has imposed sanctions on various PRC "entities" (including state-owned entities) for troublesome transfers related to missiles and chemical weapons to Pakistan, Iran, or perhaps another country, including repeated sanctions on some "serial proliferators." Since 2009, the Obama Administration has imposed sanctions on 16 occasions on multiple entities in China for weapons proliferation.

Skeptics question whether China's roles in weapons nonproliferation warrant a closer relationship with China, even as sanctions were required on some PRC technology transfers. Some criticize the imposition of U.S. sanctions targeting PRC "entities" but not the government. Others doubt the effectiveness of any stress on sanctions over diplomacy or a comprehensive strategy. Concerns grew that China expanded nuclear cooperation with Pakistan, supported North Korea, and could undermine sanctions against Iran (including in the oil/gas energy sector). In 2002-2008, the U.S. approach relied on China's influence on North Korea to dismantle its nuclear weapons. Beijing hosted the Six-Party Talks (last held in December 2008) with limited results. Since 2006, China's balanced approach has evolved to vote for some U.N. Security Council (UNSC) sanctions against missile or nuclear proliferation in North Korea and Iran. Some called for engaging more with Beijing to use its leverage against Pyongyang and Tehran. However, North Korea's nuclear tests in 2006, 2009, and 2013 prompted greater debate about how to change China's calculus and the value of its cooperation. After negotiations, the PRC voted in June 2009 for UNSC Resolution 1874 to expand sanctions imposed under Resolution 1718 in 2006 against North Korea. The PRC voted in June 2010 for UNSC Resolution 1929 for the fourth set of sanctions against Iran. In 2013, the PRC voted for UNSC Resolutions 2087 and 2094 on North Korea for missile and nuclear tests. Still, China has continued its balanced approach that includes incremental implementation of UNSC sanctions. China's approach has not shown fundamental changes toward Pakistan, Iran, and North Korea. China again is calling for resuming the Six-Party Talks, but the Administration says the goal is North Korea's credible denuclearization. On November 29, 2013, the Secretary of State again announced that China (and other countries) "significantly" reduced crude oil imports from Iran and that sanctions under the FY2012 National Defense Authorization Act (NDAA) (P.L. 112-81) would not apply. Legislation includes H.Res. 65 (Royce), H.R. 673 (Ros-Lehtinen), and S. 298 (Menendez). In December, Congress passed the NDAA for FY2014, **H.R. 3304**, with Section 1248 to require a report on a plan to reduce missile proliferation in Iran, North Korea, and Syria, including with the PRC's cooperation.

Contents

Tables

Contacts

Purpose and Scope

Congress has long been concerned about whether U.S. policy advances U.S. security interests in reducing the role of the People's Republic of China (PRC) in the proliferation of weapons of mass destruction (WMD) and missiles as well as obtaining China's cooperation in weapons nonproliferation. This problem refers to the threat of nuclear, chemical, or biological weapons and missiles that could deliver them. Some have argued that certain PRC transfers violated international treaties or guidelines, and/or have contravened various U.S. laws requiring sanctions to shore up those international standards. Even if no laws or treaties are violated, many view China's transfers as threatening U.S. security interests. Using unclassified consultations and citations, this CRS Report discusses the national security problem of the PRC's role in weapons proliferation and issues related to the U.S. policy response, including legislation. **Table 1**, at the end of this report, summarizes the U.S. sanctions imposed or waived on PRC entities or the PRC government for weapons proliferation. For a discussion of the policy problem in the 1980s to 1996, see CRS Report 96-767, *Chinese Proliferation of Weapons of Mass Destruction: Background and Analysis*, and CRS Report 98-485, *China: Possible Missile Technology Transfers Under U.S. Satellite Export Policy—Actions and Chronology*, by Shirley A. Kan.

PRC Proliferation Challenges

Partial Nonproliferation Commitments

Since 1991, Beijing has taken steps to address U.S. and other countries' concerns by increasing its partial participation in international nonproliferation regimes and issuing export control regulations. However, questions have remained. China first promised tentatively to abide by the Missile Technology Control Regime (MTCR) in November 1991 and February 1992 and later reaffirmed that commitment in an October 4, 1994, joint statement with the United States. The MTCR, set up in 1987, is not an international agreement and has no legal authority, leaving issues about U.S. sanctions to shore up the standards unresolved. It is a set of voluntary guidelines that seeks to control the transfer of ballistic and cruise missiles that are inherently capable of delivering at least a 500 kg (1,100 lb) payload to at least 300 km (186 mi), called Category I or MTCR-class missiles. It was unclear whether China adhered to the revised MTCR guidelines of 1993 calling for the presumption to deny transfers of *any* missiles capable of delivering *any* WMD (not just nuclear weapons). A 1996 State Department fact sheet said that China unilaterally committed to controlling exports "consistent with the MTCR Guidelines and Annex," with the MTCR consisting of a common export control policy (*Guidelines*) applied to a common list of controlled items (*Annex*). However, a Senate Foreign Relations Committee report of September 11, 2000, said the State Department had argued to Congress that China agreed to the MTCR Guidelines, but not the Annex.

On November 21, 2000, Beijing said that it has no intention of assisting any other country in developing ballistic missiles that can be used to deliver nuclear weapons (missiles with payloads of at least 500 kg and ranges of at least 300 km) and promised to issue missile-related export controls "as soon as possible." After a contentious period that saw new U.S. sanctions, the PRC finally published those regulations and the control list (modeled on the MTCR) on August 25, 2002, as Washington and Beijing prepared for a Bush-Jiang summit on October 25, 2002. In 2004, China applied to join the MTCR but has not been accepted as a member.

China acceded to the Nuclear Nonproliferation Treaty (NPT) on March 9, 1992. The NPT does not ban peaceful nuclear projects. On May 11, 1996, the PRC issued a statement promising to make only safeguarded nuclear transfers. China, on July 30, 1996, began a moratorium on nuclear testing and signed the Comprehensive Test Ban Treaty (CTBT) in September 1996 but (like the United States) has not ratified it. Premier Li Peng issued nuclear export control regulations on September 10, 1997. On October 16, 1997, China joined the Zangger Committee (on nuclear trade). Also in October 1997, China promised not to start new nuclear cooperation with Iran. On June 6, 1998, the U.N. Security Council (including China) adopted Resolution 1172, asking states to prevent exports to India or Pakistan's nuclear weapon or missile programs. The PRC issued regulations on dual-use nuclear exports on June 17, 1998. In May 2004, China applied to join the Nuclear Suppliers Group (NSG), which accepted China as a member after the Bush Administration decided to support China, despite congressional concerns.

In 1995, China issued its first public defense white paper, which focused on arms control and disarmament. Also, China signed the Chemical Weapons Convention (CWC) in January 1993. On April 25, 1997, China deposited its instrument of ratification of the CWC, before it entered into force on April 29, 1997. From 1993 to 1998, the PRC issued export control regulations on chemicals. On October 14, 2002, on the eve of a Bush-Jiang summit, the PRC issued regulations for export controls over dual-use biological agents and related technology. On December 3, 2003, China issued a white paper on nonproliferation, which stated that its control lists are almost the same as those of the Zangger Committee, NSG, CWC, Australia Group, and MTCR.

Continuing Concerns and Intelligence Report

Nevertheless, China is not a member of the MTCR or the Australia Group (AG) (on chemical and biological weapons). (In June 2004, China expressed willingness to join the MTCR.) China did not join the 93 countries in signing the International Code of Conduct Against Ballistic Missile Proliferation in The Hague on November 25, 2002. China has not joined the Proliferation Security Initiative (PSI) announced by President Bush on May 31, 2003. PRC weapons proliferation has persisted, aggravating trends that result in more ambiguous technical assistance (vs. transfers of hardware), longer range missiles, more indigenous capabilities, and secondary (i.e., retransferred) proliferation.

The Director of Central Intelligence (DCI) noted that, for July-December 1996, "China was the most significant supplier of WMD-related goods and technology to foreign countries." As required by Section 721 of the FY1997 Intelligence Authorization Act (P.L. 104-293), the intelligence community's report to Congress, "Unclassified Report to Congress on the Acquisition of Technology Relating to Weapons of Mass Destruction and Advanced Conventional Munitions," named "entities" in China (plus North Korea and Russia) as **key suppliers** of dangerous technology that could contribute to WMD and missile programs. China's "entities," including state-owned defense industrial corporations, were reported to be "associated" with Pakistan's nuclear and missile programs and Iran's missile programs. Subsequent discussions of this required report refer to this **Section 721 Report**. Original legislation required a semi-annual report. The FY2004 Intelligence Authorization Act (P.L. 108-177) changed the requirement for an annual report. The Director of National Intelligence (DNI) submitted to Congress the latest unclassified Section 721 Report to cover the year of 2011. The Intelligence Authorization Act for FY2013 (P.L. 112-277) repealed this reporting requirement (Sec. 310).

Nuclear Technology Sales to Pakistan

Overview

In 1996, U.S. policymakers faced the issue of whether to impose sanctions on the PRC for technology transfers to Pakistan's nuclear program, and Beijing issued another nuclear nonproliferation pledge. Since then, the United States has maintained concerns—but at a lower level—about continued PRC nuclear cooperation with Pakistan, particularly involving the construction of nuclear power plants. The PRC government likely has known about the nuclear cooperation with Pakistan. Nonetheless, in 2004, the Bush Administration supported China's application to join the Nuclear Suppliers Group (NSG), despite congressional concerns about China's failure to apply the NSG's "full-scope safeguards" to its nuclear projects in Pakistan. (Full-scope safeguards apply IAEA inspections to all other declared nuclear facilities in addition to the facility importing supplies in order to prevent diversions to weapon programs.) The Obama Administration has not raised strong concerns about the PRC's expansion of nuclear projects.

Nuclear Cooperation

Concerns have persisted about PRC assistance to Pakistan's nuclear facilities. As reported by Pakistani and PRC news sources in 1992, China began to build a nuclear power plant at Chashma and was suspected in 1994 of helping Pakistan to build an unsafeguarded, plutonium-producing reactor at Khushab, according to *Nucleonics Week* (June 19, 1997, and February 26, 1998). Operational since 2001, the Chashma reactor has IAEA safeguards but not full scope safeguards (*Nucleonics Week*, April 26, 2001; and IAEA, *Annual Report 2001*).

Referring specifically to Pakistan's efforts to acquire equipment, materials, and technology for its nuclear weapons program, the DCI's June 1997 Section 721 report for the last half of 1996 (after China's May 1996 pledge) stated that China was the "principal supplier." Then, on May 11 and 13, 1998, India conducted nuclear tests, citing China's nuclear ties to Pakistan, and Pakistan followed with nuclear tests on May 28 and 30, 1998. China, as Pakistan's principal military and nuclear supplier, failed to avert the tests and did not cut off nuclear aid, but condemned the tests at the U.N. The U.S. Arms Control and Disarmament Agency's annual report on arms control for 1998 stated that "there continued to be some contacts between Chinese entities and Pakistan's unsafeguarded and nuclear weapons program."

In 2000, news reports said that some former U.S. nonproliferation and intelligence officials suspected that China provided equipment for Pakistan's secret heavy water production plant at Khushab, where an unsafeguarded reactor reportedly started up in April 1998 and generated weapons-grade plutonium. Clinton Administration officials at the White House and State Department reportedly denied China's involvement but said that they did not know the origins of the plant.[1] The DCI reported in November 2003 that, in the first half of 2003, continued contacts between PRC entities and "entities associated with Pakistan's nuclear weapons program" cannot be ruled out, despite the PRC's 1996 promise not to assist unsafeguarded nuclear facilities. The Director of the Defense Intelligence Agency (DIA), Vice Admiral Lowell Jacoby, testified to the Senate Intelligence Committee on February 24, 2004, that PRC entities "remain involved with

---

[1] Mark Hibbs, "CIA Knew About Khushab D2O Plant but Not Source, Officials Claim," *Nucleonics Week*, March 23, 2000; "Pakistani Separation Plant Now Producing 8-10 Kg Plutonium/Yr," *Nuclear Fuel*, June 12, 2000.

nuclear and missile programs in Pakistan and Iran," while "in some cases," the entities were involved without the government's knowledge, thus implying that there were cases in which the PRC government had knowledge of the relationships.

On May 5, 2004, China signed a contract to build a second nuclear power reactor (Chashma-2) in Pakistan. This contract raised questions because of continuing PRC nuclear cooperation with Pakistan and its signing right before a decision by the Nuclear Suppliers Group (NSG) on China's membership, applied with U.S. support. With a pre-existing contract, Chashma-2 was exempted from the NSG's requirement for full-scope safeguards (not just IAEA safeguards on the reactor).[2] (See "Nonproliferation Regimes (MTCR, NSG, etc.)" below for policy discussion.)

After China's grandfathering of the Chashma-2 reactor under a pre-existing contract, the United States and other countries monitored China's subsequent agreement in October 2008 to build two more nuclear reactors in Pakistan for compliance with the NSG's rules, unless there would be an exemption (like that for India in 2008). In February 2010, China tentatively agreed to finance construction of two more reactors (Chashma-3 and Chashma-4), and the next month, Pakistan's government approved the deal in which the PRC promised a loan for the projects. In June, PRC companies reportedly promised to build the reactors.[3] The PRC acknowledged the deal and contended that the reactors would be subject to IAEA safeguards. However, when President Obama met with PRC leader Hu Jintao and hosted the Nuclear Security Summit in Washington on April 12 and 13, 2010, briefings did not mention discussion of this dispute involving China and Pakistan. Later, Assistant Secretary of State for South and Central Asian Affairs Robert Blake said in Beijing on May 4 that China's deal would require it to seek an exception to the NSG's guidelines. Acting Assistant Secretary of State for International Security and Nonproliferation Vann Van Diepen testified that the Administration decided to vote against an exemption for China, at a hearing on July 22 of the House Foreign Affairs Subcommittee on Terrorism, Nonproliferation, and Trade. On September 21, the PRC Foreign Ministry claimed that the 3rd and 4th reactors were "based on" the PRC-Pakistan agreement signed in 2003 and that China requested IAEA safeguards.

Relatedly, on December 21, 2010, PPG Paints Trading Company in Shanghai pled guilty in a U.S. court to illegally exporting high-performance coatings from the United States through the PRC to the Chashma-2 reactor in Pakistan from June 2006 to March 2007. Later, on June 16, 2011, authorities in Atlanta arrested Wang Xun, a PRC national and U.S. resident. On November 16, the Commerce Department ordered sanctions against Wang. On December 3, 2012, the China Nuclear Industry Huaxing Construction Company of Nanjing pled guilty in a U.S. criminal case for illegal exports of high-performance epoxy coatings from the United States to the Chashma-2 reactor. The Section 721 Report for 2011 continued to report that PRC entities as associated with Pakistan's nuclear programs.

In another visit to Beijing on March 17-18, 2011, Assistant Secretary of State Blake reiterated the U.S. expectation for China to abide by the NSG's guidelines as committed by China when it became a member in 2004. He stated that construction of new nuclear reactors (e.g., Chashma-3 and Chashma-4) would be "inconsistent" with China's obligations to the NSG. Nonetheless, he balanced that criticism by also expressing support for Pakistan in meeting its energy needs.

---

[2] "Pakistan, China Agree on Second Chashma Unit," *Nucleonics Week*, May 6, 2004.

[3] *Daily Times*, Lahore, October 19; *Nucleonics Week*, October 23; *Jane's Defense Weekly*, October 29, 2008; *Daily Times*, Lahore, March 30, 2010; *Financial Times*, April 29, 2010; *Reuters*, June 24, 2010.

However, the Carnegie Endowment argued in 2011 that two more reactors from China in six or more years would cover only 20% of Pakistan's electricity shortfall and that the design lacked modern safety standards.[4] When the Obama Administration held another Strategic and Economic Dialogue (S&ED) with the PRC on May 9-10, U.S. officials did not raise publicly this dispute. Pakistan inaugurated Chashma-2's operations on May 12, 2011. In 2013, China reportedly signed the formal agreement in February to build Chashma-3. China also expanded nuclear cooperation, reportedly promising to build two nuclear power reactors in Karachi with a loan for $6.5 billion. However, Prime Minister Nawaz Sharif still stressed Pakistan's energy shortages, in a visit to Shanghai in July, while Pakistan's nuclear power generated only 6% of electricity (in 2011).[5]

A. Q. Khan's Nuclear Network

China's past and persisting connections to Pakistan's nuclear program raised questions about whether China was involved in or had knowledge about the long-time efforts, publicly confirmed in early 2004, of Abdul Qadeer Khan, the former head of Pakistan's nuclear weapon program, in selling uranium enrichment technology to Iran, North Korea, and Libya. DCI George Tenet confirmed A.Q. Khan's network of nuclear trade in open testimony to the Senate Intelligence Committee on February 24, 2004.

China's ties to the network was a concern, particularly because China was an early recipient of the uranium enrichment technology using centrifuges that Khan had acquired in Europe. In return, in 1982, China gave Pakistan 15 tons of uranium hexafluoride gas for production of bomb-grade uranium, 50 kilograms of weapons-grade enriched uranium enough for two bombs, and a blue-print for a nuclear weapon that China already tested, according to Khan.[6]

Also, there were questions about whether China shared intelligence with the United States about Khan's nuclear technology transfers. With the troubling disclosures, China could have been more willing to cooperate on nonproliferation or could have been reluctant to confirm its involvement. A senior Pakistani diplomat was quoted as saying that, while in Beijing in 2002, PRC officials said they knew "A.Q. Khan was in China and bribing people, and they wanted him out."[7] Particularly troubling was the reported intelligence finding in early 2004 that Khan sold Libya a nuclear bomb design that he received from China in the early 1980s (in return for giving China his centrifuge technology), a design that China had already tested in 1966 and had developed as a compact nuclear bomb for delivery on a missile.[8] That finding raised the additional question of whether Khan also sold that bomb design to others, including Iran and North Korea. According to two former U.S. nuclear bomb designers, the PRC proliferated nuclear bomb technology to

[4] Toby Dalton, Mark Hibbs, and George Perkovich, "A Criteria-Based Approach to Nuclear Cooperation with Pakistan," Carnegie Endowment for International Peace, June 22, 2011.

[5] *Free Beacon*, March 22; *Kyodo*, June 13; *South China Morning Post*, June 25; *Nation*, July 7; *Wall Street Journal*, October 15; *Xinhua*, November 26; PRC Foreign Ministry, December 23; *Reuters*, December 24, 2013.

[6] David Sanger and William Broad, "From Rogue Nuclear Programs, Web of Trails Leads to Pakistan," *New York Times*, January 4, 2004; Simon Henderson, "Investigation: Nuclear Scandal, Dr Abdul Qadeer Khan," *Sunday Times*, London, September 20, 2009; R. Jeffrey Smith and Joby Warrick, "A Nuclear Power's Act of Proliferation," *Washington Post*, November 13, 2009.

[7] Barton Gellman and Dafna Linzer, "Unprecedented Peril Forces Tough Calls," *Washington Post*, October 26, 2004.

[8] Joby Warrick and Peter Slevin, "Libyan Arms Designs Traced Back to China," *Washington Post*, February 15, 2004; William Broad and David Sanger, "As Nuclear Secrets Emerge in Khan Inquiry, More Are Suspected," *New York Times*, December 26, 2004.

Pakistan, including a test conducted in 1990 for Pakistan of its first nuclear bomb.[9] DCI Porter Goss testified in February 2005 that the Bush Administration continued to explore opportunities to learn about Khan's nuclear trade, adding that "getting to the end of that trail is extremely important for us. It is a serious proliferation question."[10] In his memoir of 2007, George Tenet wrote that Khan's broad international network included China, North Korea, and—vaguely—"the Muslim world."[11] Finally, on January 12, 2009, the State Department imposed sanctions on 13 people and three companies for involvement in A.Q. Khan's network that proliferated nuclear technology to Iran, Libya, and North Korea. But the State Department did not name China among a number of countries that cooperated to investigate and shut down that proliferation network.

Missile Technology Sales to Pakistan

Overview

From the early 1990s to 2000, the George H. W. Bush and Clinton Administrations faced the issue of whether to impose sanctions on PRC "entities" Moreover, China's own for transferring M-11 short-range ballistic missiles or related technology to Pakistan. The Clinton Administration took eight years to determine in 2000 that PRC entities had transferred complete M-11 missiles as well as technology to Pakistan, but waived sanctions in return for another missile nonproliferation pledge from Beijing. However, despite that promise of November 2000, the United States has continued concerns about PRC technology transfers that have helped Pakistan to build domestic missile programs, including development of medium-range ballistic missiles. In September 2001, the George W. Bush Administration imposed sanctions for PRC proliferation of missile technology to Pakistan, denying satellite exports to China. While China promised not to transfer *missiles*, it has reportedly helped Pakistan to achieve an indigenous missile capability.

Despite the PRC's November 2000 missile nonproliferation pledge, in the first several months of 2001, a PRC company reportedly delivered 12 shipments of missile components to Pakistan's Shaheen-1 SRBM and Shaheen-2 MRBM programs, according to the *Washington Times* (August 6, 2001). On September 1, 2001, the State Department imposed sanctions on China Metallurgical Equipment Corporation (CMEC) for proliferation of missile technology (Category II items of the MTCR) to Pakistan. In November 2004, the DCI told Congress in a Section 721 report that, in the second half of 2003, PRC entities helped Pakistan to advance toward serial production of solid-fuel SRBMs (previously identified as the Shaheen-1, Abdali, and Ghaznavi) and supported Pakistan's development of solid-fuel MRBMs (previously noted as the Shaheen-2 MRBM). The DNI's Section 721 Report for 2011 reported that PRC entities continued to supply missile-related items to Pakistan. Though that report stressed that they were "primarily" private entities, entities could include state-owned organizations. The report also stressed entities, not the regime.

---

[9] Thomas Reed, "The Chinese Nuclear Tests, 1964-1996," *Physics Today*, September 2008; Alex Kingsbury, "Why China Helped Countries Like Pakistan, North Korea Build Bombs," *U.S. News & World Report*, January 5, 2009. Also see R. Jeffrey Smith, "Pakistani Says N. Korea Paid Bribes for Nuclear Expertise," *Washington Post*, July 7, 2011.

[10] Senate Select Committee on Intelligence, hearing on "Global Intelligence Challenges 2005: Meeting Long-term Challenges with a Long-term Strategy," February 16, 2005.

[11] George Tenet, *At the Center of the Storm: My Years at the CIA* (Harper Collins Publishers, 2007).

Nuclear Technology Sales to Iran

Overview and Policy Approaches

In the mid-1990s, the Clinton Administration urged China to cancel ostensibly civilian nuclear projects in Iran. In negotiations leading up to the 1997 U.S.-PRC summit, China pledged to end nuclear cooperation with Iran. At the summit, President Clinton promised to implement the 1985 U.S.-PRC nuclear cooperation agreement (to sell nuclear power reactors to China). However, the United States was concerned about whether China abided by its October 1997 promise. With revelations in 2002 about Iran's uranium enrichment program, the Bush Administration in 2004 sought PRC support for sanctions imposed by the **U.N. Security Council** (**UNSC**), where the PRC has power to vote in favor, abstain, or veto. The PRC's position has evolved to support some sanctions but not use of force. The PRC voted for **UNSC Resolutions 1737 (2006), 1747 (2007), 1803 (2008), and 1929 (2010)** to impose sanctions on Iran. However, the PRC also has invested in and traded with Iran's oil and gas energy sector.

As complementary or alternative approaches, some have viewed China's cooperation in pressuring Iran as necessarily for a working U.S.-PRC relationship, especially through the use of summits. Others have focused attention on sanctions to target Iran's energy-related investments, industries, and imports. An alternative would be to prevent transfers of Western technology to Iran for developing its oil and gas industries. Diplomatic impasses have raised the burden on China's preferred dialogue to produce results in support of nonproliferation and stability in the Middle East. China likely fears greater instability or conflict in the Mideast, the source of about 50% of China's oil imports. China has tried to maintain a balanced position in support of Iran and U.S./European Union concerns, but also has evolved to support negotiations, the IAEA's authority in Iran, as well as some UNSC sanctions on Iran. Meanwhile, China pressed the United States to talk directly with Iran. After the United States shifted to hold direct dialogue with Iran without resulting in resolution of the dispute, the burden became greater on China to place a higher priority on nonproliferation than business as usual (including energy deals), by pressuring Iran or showing results of dialogue. Another approach has looked at options to alleviate China's dependence on Iranian oil through imports from other countries. Reportedly, in 2009, the Obama Administration discussed with Saudi Arabia and United Arab Emirates (UAE) about raising their supplies of oil to meet China's need, but China refused an explicit deal. Yet another option would increase China's access to investments in U.S. or other Western energy projects.[12] Still, others have viewed multilateral approaches as more critical in dealing with Beijing. More significant Russian nuclear cooperation with Iran has offered China maneuvering room in diplomacy. However, any closer Russian alignment with the United States and European countries would increase China's isolation at the UNSC. In addition to the three tracks supported by China (involving dialogue with Iran, the IAEA, and some UNSC sanctions), the United States, European and Asian allies, and Israel have options of sanctions separate from those imposed by the UNSC and the use of force (that would not require China's vote). Also, Congress and the Administration could urge allies and partners to suspend trade in Iran's oil and gasoline.

In the February 2001 Section 721 Report (on the first half of 2000), the DCI dropped an earlier observation that the 1997 pledge appeared to be holding. In testimony before the Senate Governmental Affairs Subcommittee on International Security, Proliferation, and Federal Services

---

[12] *Guardian*, August 25; *Wall Street Journal*, October 20; *Haaretz*, December 17, 2009; *Reuters*, October 28, 2010.

on June 6, 2002, Assistant Secretary of State John Wolf stated concerns about possible PRC-Iranian interactions "despite China's 1997 pledge to end its nuclear cooperation with Iran."

Uranium Enrichment

In 2002, an Iranian opposition group revealed that Iranian front companies procured materials from China (and other countries) for secret nuclear weapons facilities, while experts from China worked at a uranium mine at Saghand and a centrifuge facility (for uranium enrichment) near Isfahan, reported the *Washington Post* (December 19, 2002, and February 20, 2003). Moreover, *Nucleonics Week* (February 27 and March 6, 2003) reported that Iran, since 2000, was building a secret uranium enrichment plant at Natanz with technology for gas centrifuge enrichment from Pakistan (Khan Research Laboratories), a country that has received nuclear cooperation from China. Also, the IAEA found out in 2003 that, in 1991, China supplied Iran with 1.8 metric tons of natural uranium, reported *Nucleonics Week* (June 12, 2003). The head of the Iranian Atomic Organization reported an Iranian-PRC contract to extract uranium ore in Yazd.[13] The DCI's Section 721 Report (issued in November 2004) confirmed that the Iranian opposition group, "beginning in August of 2002, revealed several previously undisclosed Iranian nuclear facilities."

Testifying to Congress on February 11, 2003, DCI George Tenet pointed to China's "firms" (rather than the government) and warned that they "may be backing away from Beijing's 1997 bilateral commitment to forego any new nuclear cooperation with Iran." The DCI's Section 721 Report of November 2003 reported that "some interactions of concern" between PRC and Iranian entities continued in the first half of 2003. The Director of the Defense Intelligence Agency, Vice Admiral Lowell Jacoby, testified to the Senate Intelligence Committee on February 24, 2004, that PRC entities "remain involved with nuclear and missile programs in Pakistan and Iran, while, "in some cases," the entities are involved without the PRC government's knowledge. Then, in April 2004, the Administration imposed sanctions under the Iran Nonproliferation Act. Assistant Secretary of State John Wolf testified to the House International Relations Committee on May 18, 2004, that "most" of the sanctions related to non-nuclear transfers, but there were concerns in the nuclear area as well.

In May 2006, diplomatic sources revealed that Iran had used uranium hexafluoride gas (UF6) from China to accelerate Iran's uranium enrichment program. An Iranian news agency acknowledged that hexafluoride from China was used in initial uranium enrichment, after which domestic supplies were applied.[14]

China's companies reportedly have helped Iran to procure nuclear-related hardware. In 2007, a PRC company in Dalian supplied Iran with sensitive materials for its nuclear program, including graphite, tungsten copper, tungsten powder, and high-strength aluminum alloys and maraging steel. In March 2009, the Shanghai-based Roc-Master Manufacture and Supply Company ordered 108 pressure gauges that could be used in centrifuges to enrich uranium for transfer to Iran from an agent in Taiwan (Heli-Ocean Technology Company) for Inficon Holding, the manufacturer in Switzerland. In 2010, under an IAEA investigation, China's Zhejiang Ouhai Trade Corporation, a subsidiary of Jinzhou Group, supplied to Iran sensitive valves and vacuum gauges useful for uranium enrichment and made by KD Valves-Descote in France. The reported recipient in Iran

---

[13] *Mehr News Agency*, Tehran, December 10, 2004.

[14] "Iran Using Chinese-made Feedstock for Enriched Uranium: Diplomats," *AFP*, May 18, 2006; *Iranian Students News Agency*, May 19, 2006.

was Javedan Mehr Toos, a firm procuring nuclear-related items for Kalaye Electric Company that is part of the Atomic Energy Organization of Iran. The French firm denied selling its sensitive products to China, and the PRC company denied the story.[15] On June 16, 2010, the Department of the Treasury imposed sanctions on Javedan Mehr Toos among Iran's entities, individuals, and ships subject to U.S. sanctions under Executive Order 13382 for WMD proliferation.

Dual Approach and Energy-related Oil and Gas Deals

Since 2004, the United States has sought China's cooperation (with its veto power) at the IAEA and U.N. to achieve the U.S. and European objective of containing Iran's suspected nuclear weapon program by having the IAEA refer Iran's case to the UNSC for sanctions in response to Iran's suspected violation of the NPT. The talks are called **P5+1** referring to the five permanent members of the UNSC plus Germany, or **E3+3,** referring to the three European Union countries of Britain, France, and Germany plus the United States, Russia, and China. While it might share U.S. concerns about nuclear nonproliferation, China has expressed reservations about sanctions and the credibility of some U.S. intelligence. Moreover, China's own "entities" have supplied sensitive technology to Iran. Beijing has interests in raising its leverage vis-à-vis Washington, including to check U.S. dominance and support for Taiwan.

Meanwhile, China has a competing priority of economic ties with Iran to fuel economic growth partly with global investments, and China generally opposes sanctions that target energy deals. There are concerns that China's economic interests and influence in Iran, including multi-billion-dollar oil and gas deals, could undermine U.S., European, and Asian pressure on and isolation of Iran, and that China could capitalize on other countries' sanctions by filling in situations where U.S., European, and Asian companies pull back from investments in or supplies to Iran. The PRC has not announced formal unilateral sanctions on Iran's energy sector or support for those of other countries. Any PRC exploitation of sanctions for gains could unravel international solidarity.

Oil. PRC companies, such as Sinopec and Zhuhai Zhenrong Corporation, reportedly have imported crude oil from Iran. In early 2012, as other countries reduced trade with Iran, China's companies like SINOPEC reportedly used their increased leverage and cut oil imports from Iran. However, the cut was due to commercial negotiations over prices and payment terms. China also increased oil imports from other countries, showing it could diversify away from Iranian oil if willing to do so. When PRC Premier Wen Jiabao visited Saudi Arabia in January 2012, its officials reportedly raised concerns about Iran and offered to expand oil supplies to China. By the end of 2011, China imported about 555,000 barrels per day (bpd) of Iranian crude oil. The PRC's import of crude oil from Iran dropped by 21% from 2011 to 2012, back to a level slightly above that in 2010. Iran was the fourth-largest foreign supplier of crude oil to China (after Saudi Arabia, Angola, and Russia). Iranian oil accounted for 8% of China's oil imports. In January-October 2013, China's import of Iranian crude oil dropped 3% from last year's same period. However, while China has cut its import of crude oil from Iran, China has increased significantly its import of fuel oil from Iran, using a loophole in sanctions and giving Iran some important revenue.[16]

---

[15] Peter Enav and Debby Wu, "How Nuclear Equipment Reached Iran," *AP*, February 28, 2010; Verna Yu, "Mainland Firm Denies Breaking Sanctions on Iran," *South China Morning Post*, March 2, 2010; Peter Fritsch and David Crawford, "Western Authorities Investigate China Connection in Export of French Valves," *Wall Street Journal*, April 3, 2010; James Areddy, "China Firm Denies Iran Nuclear Role," *WSJ*, April 15, 2010; John Pomfret, "U.S. Says Chinese Businesses and Banks Are Bypassing U.N. Sanctions Against Iran," *Washington Post*, October 18, 2010.

[16] *Wall Street Journal*, August 21 and October 24, 2013.

Investments. PRC state-owned companies like Sinopec and China National Petroleum Corporation (CNPC) have invested significantly in Iran's oil and gas sector. China's companies reportedly promised investments totaling about $55 billion in Iran's energy industries by the end of 2009. However, committed funds would be difficult to confirm. Moreover, progress has depended on acquiring gas liquefaction technology that China has lacked. CNPC's Huanqiu Contracting and Engineering Corporation planned to build a natural gas liquefaction plant by 2016. In November 2010, China's ENN Energy Trading Company signed a deal with a U.S. company, Cheniere Energy Partners, to export U.S. liquefied natural gas (LNG) to China. Starting in 2007 or 2009, hackers based in China reportedly conducted a cyberespionage campaign, that McAfee called Night Dragon, to target major Western energy companies.[17]

The PRC's investments include the following significant projects. In October 2004, China and Iran signed a memorandum of understanding to develop Iran's Yadavaran oil field in a project initially worth $70 billion. Amid ongoing negotiations between China's Sinopec and Iran, this potential venture was valued at up to $100 billion in early 2006. In December 2007, Sinopec signed the contract to invest about $2 billion to develop the Yadavaran oil field, and the State Department responded that it was deeply disappointed and disturbed at this deal. In addition to Sinopec, the China National Offshore Oil Corporation (CNOOC) and an Iranian company signed a memorandum of understanding in December 2006 involving an investment from China worth $16 billion to produce LNG at the North Pars gas field. With a delay in further commitment, CNOOC reportedly signed the contract in May 2009. In January 2007, CNPC announced an investment of $3.6 billion to develop Phase 14 at Iran's South Pars gas field. (In 2007, Royal Dutch Shell (headquartered in the Netherlands) and Repsol (based in Spain) considered a deal to develop Phases 13 and 14 at South Pars. In June 2010, the two European companies withdrew from the project and committed to the United States not to hold further talks with Iran. At that time, the Iranian Revolutionary Guard Corps reportedly got involved in those two phases among others at South Pars.) In the presence of the PRC ambassador, CNPC also signed a contract worth $1.8 billion in January 2009 to develop Iran's North Azadegan oil field, and the PRC Foreign Ministry called the deal "normal energy cooperation." In March 2009, China's HuaFu Engineering Company signed a contract apparently to invest $3.2 billion to produce LNG at Phase 12 of the South Pars gas field. Then in June, CNPC signed a contract worth $4.7 billion to develop Phase 11 of South Pars, reportedly replacing Total of France. In August 2009, a state-owned insurance company, likely Sinosure, reportedly indicated an investment of $11.3 billion in Iran's oil refineries. China's Sinopec reportedly agreed in a memorandum of understanding in November 2009 to invest $6.5 billion in Iran's refineries to reduce its dependence on imported gasoline. Japan had concerns about China taking over an investment in the South Azadegan oilfield, with reports that China National Petroleum Corporation International (CNPCI) gained 70% share in September 2009 after Japan's Inpex company reduced its stake from 75% in 2004 to 10% in 2006. Since 2009, CNPC reportedly has considered an investment of most or all of $2.5 billion. Inpex decided in September 2010 to withdraw from South Azadegan.[18]

---

[17] *Reuters*, August 18, 2010, January 14, 2011; *Wall Street Journal*, February 10 and February 14, 2011.

[18] Numerous sources include *Wall Street Journal* and *Washington Post*, February 17, 2006; *China Daily*, January 6, 2007; *AFP*, January 11 and 15, 2007; *Fars News Agency*, January 16, 2007; *Reuters*, January 29, 2007; *Vision of the Islamic Republic of Iran Network*, December 9, 2007; *Reuters*, December 10, 2007; *Dongfang Zaobao*, December 11, 2007; *Xinhua*, January 14, 2009; *AP*, March 14, 2009; *Upstream*, March 20, 2009; *Global Insight*, May 29, 2009; *Reuters*, June 3 and 4, 2009; *Tehran Times*, August 30, 2009; *Iran Daily*, August 31, 2009; *Al-Manar TV Online*, June 15, 2010; *Taiwan News*, June 15, 2010; *Jiji Press*, September 30, 2010.

Gasoline. Regarding China's gasoline supplies, Zhuhai Zhenrong (and possibly others) reportedly started in 2008 to sell gasoline through intermediaries to Iran, supplying one-third of its imports by September 2009. Further, in early 2010, a PRC state-owned company, Chinaoil, sent two shipments of gasoline in the company's first direct exports to Iran since January 2009, and Sinopec also planned to sell gasoline to Iran. In August 2010, China's Zhuhai Zhenrong in partnership with Russia's LUKOIL exported gasoline to Iran. (Lukoil re-committed the next month to cease gasoline exports to Iran.) By then, PRC supplies of gasoline to Iran reached about one-half of its imports. Zhuhai Zhenrong is a state-owned trading enterprise, set up in 1994 not only by the PRC's State Council (like a Cabinet) but also the Central Military Commission (high command of the People's Liberation Army). The firm has worked with Iran's Ministries of Defense and Oil. Another PRC state-owned enterprise, ZhenHua Oil, reportedly started to supply gasoline to Iran in 2009, providing up to one-third of Iran's imports by early 2010. ZhenHua Oil was set up in 2003 as a subsidiary of China North Industries Corporation (NORINCO), a defense industrial conglomerate which has faced U.S. sanctions (see **Table 1** at the end of this report). In early 2012, China's state-owned companies reportedly continued to ship gasoline to Iran.[19]

Since 2010, concerns increased about enforcement of U.S. sanctions against PRC companies, after enactment of the Comprehensive Iran Sanctions, Accountability, and Divestment Act (**CISADA**) of 2010 as **P.L. 111-195** on July 1, 2010, following UNSC Resolution 1929 of June. China did not replace India in the original proposal for an Iran-Pakistan-India gas pipeline, when the agreement was reached in June 2010 for the Iran-Pakistan pipeline. By March 2012, the Industrial and Commercial Bank of China (ICBC) reportedly backed out of arranging finances.[20] Still, China's companies could become contractors in the project, which started in March 2013.

However, in addition to the United States, Canada, Australia, the European Union, Japan, and South Korea imposed sanctions on Iran, and they have concerns about China's exploitation of their sanctions that restrain investments in Iran. At a press conference on August 4, 2010, the State Department's Special Advisor for Nonproliferation and Arms Control Robert Einhorn acknowledged U.S. concerns that China's companies would benefit from sanctions by taking over deals abandoned by other foreign companies in support of U.S. and other sanctions against Iran's energy sector, unilateral sanctions opposed by China for "expanding" UNSC sanctions. Einhorn said that the Obama Administration urged China to act as a "responsible stakeholder." Two days later in Beijing, PRC Vice Premier Li Keqiang met with Iran's Oil Minister, but Li discussed "existing" projects, with no reported PRC commitment to new deals. In September 2010, Einhorn then went to Beijing with a "significant list" of PRC companies and banks that were suspected of violating U.N. sanctions, with or without the PRC government's approval of deals that occurred before and after June 2010. Einhorn also urged the PRC's oil companies, such as CNPC, to stop or limit investments in Iran, at least temporarily. At the end of September, the State Department issued a "fact sheet" to commend a number of foreign energy firms for stopping activities in Iran but was not able to name any PRC energy companies. (A shipping company in Hong Kong, NYK Line, stopped trading with Iran.) Also, the State Department confirmed on October 18 that it provided information to China about "specific concerns" about some PRC "companies," and that the PRC promised to investigate the cases. However, the PRC Foreign Ministry said the next day

---

[19] *Financial Times*, September 22, 2009; *Reuters*, September 23, 2009; *Mehr News*, September 29, 2009; *Reuters*, November 25, 2009; *Financial Times*, March 7, 2010; *Reuters*, April 14, 2010; *Reuters*, August 11, 2010; *Reuters*, February 27, 2012.

[20] *Express Tribune*, March 14, 2012. The next day, the PRC Foreign Ministry did not confirm or deny this news.

that it was following "the letter" of UNSC resolutions, with no mention of sanctions on Iran's energy sector or of any PRC investigations into PRC entities.

Still, by that month, the PRC government reportedly issued informal orders to its companies to slow down their work in Iran's energy projects. Apparently, CNPC suspended work at the South Azadegan oil field, the project that raised Japan's concern (as discussed above). Iran seemed to have concerns about the pace of implementation of PRC investments, when Iran's Minister of Economic Affairs and Finance announced in Beijing in April 2011 an Iran-China "oil and gas committee." The PRC government, in late 2010, reportedly told CNOOC to suspend the project at North Pars, and CNOOC withdrew its team. Sinopec delayed the start of the project at Yadavaran. On June 17, the National Iranian Oil Company threatened CNPC with domestic replacements if it continued to delay the development of Phase 11 of South Pars (after CNPC replaced Total), and CNPC reportedly spent just $18 million in the project by August 2011. Repeatedly in 2012, Iran's oil minister warned CNPC that it risked the contract's cancellation if it did not start work.[21]

As for the PRC's direct actions on U.S. information about PRC companies, Under Secretary of State William Burns testified to House Foreign Affairs Committee on December 1, 2010, that the Obama Administration took seriously all information about PRC companies and provided that information to the PRC. He acknowledged that "in some cases," the PRC acted on the information, but "the record is a mixed one," and the Administration continued to raise concerns. On the eve of top PRC ruler Hu Jintao's state visit in Washington, Secretary of State Hillary Clinton told *ABC* on January 18, 2011, that some PRC entities were still not "as in compliance" with sanctions on Iran as the United States expected, with the PRC responding that it enforced only sanctions under UNSC resolutions. She said that the United States conveyed its expectation that Beijing implement all other sanctions on Iran. Moreover, Secretary Clinton testified to the House Foreign Affairs Committee on March 1 that China did not perceive a threat from Iran. She described the U.S. challenge in a "constant, committed, and determined" daily effort to keep China's adherence even to sanctions to which it already agreed. She named five foreign firms that withdrew from energy investments in Iran (Shell, Statoil, ENI, Total, and Inpex), but she could not name any that belonged to the PRC.

Some Members in Congress raised the issue of whether the Administration would apply CISADA sanctions to PRC firms. On the eve of a PRC leader Hu Jintao's state visit, Senators Joseph Lieberman and Mark Kirk wrote a letter to President Obama on January 14, 2011, urging him to warn Hu that the United States will be forced to sanction PRC companies if they do not suspend business ties with Iran. On March 10, 10 Senators led by Senators Jon Kyl and Robert Menendez wrote to Secretary of State Clinton, stating that it appeared that PRC firms conducted significant activity in violation of U.S. law. They added that, "we cannot afford to create the impression that China will be given a free rein to conduct economic activity in Iran when more responsible nations have chosen to follow the course that we have asked of them."[22]

Among companies in the PRC, a Hong Kong shipping company, NYK Line, first announced a stop to trade with Iran, according to the State Department's statement of May 24, 2011.

---

[21] News sources included *Shana News Agency*, June 13, 2010; *Xinhua*, August 6, 2010; *Caixin Wang*, August 19, 2010; *Washington Post*, October 18, 2010; *Reuters*, October 28, 2010; *Tehran Times*, April 23, 2011; *Reuters*, June 17, 2011; *Platts Commodity News*, August 14, 2011; *Reuters*, September 2, 2011; *Mehr News Agency*, April 19, 2012; *Tehran Times*, June 25, 2012; *Press TV*, February 5, 2013.

[22] Senators Jon Kyl, Robert Menendez, Kirsten Gillibrand, Jerry Moran, Robert Casey, Jr., Roy Blunt, Lindsey Graham, Bill Nelson, Benjamin Cardin, and Marco Rubio, letter to Secretary Hillary Clinton, March 10, 2011.

Concerning sanctions under the UNSC and CISADA, Under Secretary of the Treasury for Terrorism and Financial Intelligence David Cohen traveled to Hong Kong and Beijing on September 26-28, to seek cooperation to prevent Iran from using the global financial system for its nuclear and missile programs and to stress the risk of doing business with the Islamic Republic of Iran Shipping Lines (IRISL). Cohen warned four PRC banks (Bank of China, China Construction Bank, Industrial and Commercial Bank of China, and the Agricultural Bank of China) that accepting payments from an Iranian insurer (Moallem) would cut them off from the U.S. banking system, according to *AFP*. However, the PRC Foreign Ministry's spokesman asserted that the PRC implements UNSC resolutions and has "normal business" with Iran, without referring to CISADA, banking, energy, or shipping. Waigaoqiao Shipbuilding reportedly has built oil tankers for the National Iranian Tanker Company. In July 2013, China Shipping Container Lines (CSCL) and COSCO Container Lines reportedly stopped business with Iran.

President Obama issued Executive Order 13590 on November 21, 2011, that, *inter alia*, imposed sanctions on Iran's petrochemical industry and expanded sanctions against the provision of goods, services, and technology to Iran's oil and gas business. Enacted on December 31, 2011, the National Defense Authorization Act (NDAA) for FY2012, **P.L. 112-81**, contained Section 1245 to impose sanctions on Iran's financial sector. Secretary of the Treasury Timothy Geithner then visited Beijing on January 10-11, 2012, but apparently did not reach agreement.

Sanctions. The next day, the State Department imposed the first sanctions under CISADA against China (on Zhuhai Zhenrong for supplying gasoline), though likely with limited effects. The PRC has maintained its opposition to "unilateral" sanctions against Iran and that it has "normal" economic ties with Iran separate from the nuclear program that do not violate UNSC resolutions. However, other countries have joined the United States in cutting business with Iran's energy sector, and in June 2010, China voted for UNSC Resolution 1929 (see below) which noted the link between Iran's revenues derived from its energy sector and funding of nuclear activities. On June 28, 2012, the Secretary of State stated that China "significantly reduced" oil imports from Iran and that the sanctions under P.L. 112-81 would not apply to PRC financial institutions for a potentially renewable period of 180 days. As discussed above, China cut such oil imports for its commercial interests and energy security. At the end of July, the Treasury Department imposed sanctions under CISADA (cutting off from the U.S. financial system) on CNPC's Bank of Kunlun in the PRC for continuing to handle significant international transactions for Iran's banks. The State Department denied the action was taken against China and insisted that Washington and Beijing were "on the same page," but the PRC Foreign Ministry strongly called for revocation of what it called erroneous, unwarranted sanctions that harmed the PRC's interests. (The Bank of Kunlun reportedly held $22 billion in payments for Iran's oil by November 2013, when Iran agreed on a deal with the E3+3 on its nuclear program.[23]) On December 7, 2012, June 5, 2013, and November 29, 2013, the Secretary of State again asserted that China (and other countries) reduced crude oil imports from Iran and that sanctions under P.L. 112-81 would not apply.

Congress passed the Iran Threat Reduction and Syria Human Rights Act of 2012 (**P.L. 112-158**). The law authorized further sanctions against additional forms of foreign energy dealings with Iran, including shipments of crude oil. Congress passed more sanctions in Section 1241 of the NDAA for FY2013 (**P.L. 112-239**), covering precious metals, currencies, ports, energy, shipping, and shipbuilding. (See also CRS Report RS20871, *Iran Sanctions*, by Kenneth Katzman.)

---

[23] *Tasnim*, November 2; *Reuters*, November 25, 2013.

UNSC Resolutions and Sanctions

Under U.S. and other foreign pressure, China has evolved to vote for some sanctions at the UNSC. On November 5, 2004, China's Foreign Minister Li Zhaoxing talked with Secretary of State Colin Powell, arguing that the dispute over Iran's nuclear program should remain under the IAEA's handling. On the next day, Li arrived in Tehran and opposed referral of Iran's case to the UNSC.[24] Then, at a meeting on the sideline of a U.N. summit in New York on September 13, 2005, President Bush tried to persuade PRC ruler Hu Jintao not to block the IAEA from referring Iran's case to the UNSC. Before the meeting, the Administration briefed China on U.S. classified intelligence about Iran's development of the Shahab-3 missile that could deliver a nuclear warhead. China (and others) abstained when the IAEA passed a resolution on September 24, 2005, declaring that Iran was not complying with the NPT, and the PRC envoy in Vienna continued to call for dealing with Iran at the IAEA.[25] In Beijing in November 2005, President Bush said that he had to repeat to Hu the need to stop Iran from developing nuclear weapons.[26]

The situation escalated on January 10, 2006, when Iran resumed work on uranium enrichment, after allowing IAEA inspectors to place seals on equipment at an enrichment plant at Natanz and starting negotiations with Britain, France, and Germany two years before. Deputy Secretary of State Robert Zoellick visited Beijing January 24-25, 2006, to stress the importance of the Iran problem, continue the "Senior Dialogue" over the PRC's role as a "responsible stakeholder," and discuss a summit on April 20 between PRC leader Hu Jintao and President Bush in Washington. At a news conference in Beijing on January 24, Zoellick acknowledged differences with China over "diplomatic tactics." At a special meeting in London on January 30, China, France, Germany, Russia, United Kingdom, and United States announced their agreement to "report" (rather than "refer") Iran's case to the UNSC at the special IAEA meeting in early February but to wait until March to decide at the Security Council on any actions to support the IAEA (without mentioning sanctions).[27] Still, on February 4, China was one of 27 countries that voted at the IAEA to support a resolution to report Iran to the UNSC, showing some progress in China's cooperation since it abstained on a resolution on Iran in September 2005.

When the IAEA sent a report on Iran to the UNSC on March 8, 2006, saying that it could not conclude that there were no undeclared nuclear materials or activities in Iran, China continued to be less critical of Iran and to favor the handling of this issue at the IAEA rather than the UNSC. On March 29, 2006, after weeks of negotiations, the Security Council issued a statement through its president, calling on Iran to suspend all nuclear enrichment and reprocessing activities to be verified by the IAEA and requesting an IAEA report in 30 days to the IAEA Board of Governors "and in parallel" to the Security Council, with no mention of sanctions. The Administration called for a UNSC resolution that invoked Chapter VII of the U.N. Charter (for sanctions or force), but the PRC argued against such action despite the IAEA's April 28 report on Iran's non-compliance.

On May 31, 2006, Secretary of State Rice announced U.S. support for a new approach to offer a package of incentives and costs for Iran's compliance, agreed by China and others on June 1. However, to U.S. displeasure, on June 16, the PRC hosted a summit of the Shanghai Cooperation

---

[24] *Zhongguo Wang*, October 31; *Xinhua*, November 5; *IRNA*, November 6; *Xinhua*, November 8, 2004.

[25] *New York Times*, September 14, 2005; *Wall Street Journal*, September 14, 2005; *AFP*, September 24, 2005; and *Xinhua [New China News Agency]*, September 24, 2005.

[26] George Bush, interview with Phoenix TV, based in Hong Kong, November 9, 2005.

[27] "Permanent Five Say IAEA Must Report Iran to U.N.," *Reuters*, January 31, 2006.

Organization (SCO), at which Iran attended as an observer. PRC President Hu Jintao balanced his remarks to Iranian President Ahmadinejad by saying that Iran had a right to nuclear energy and calling for its response to the offer. But with no Iranian response, on July 12, China and the other five countries issued a statement agreeing to a two-stage approach: to seek a UNSC resolution to make it mandatory for Iran to suspend nuclear enrichment as required by the IAEA; and if Iran refused, to adopt measures under Article 41 (for sanctions, not use of force) of Chapter VII.

After Iran announced that it would respond on August 22, 2006, China voted on July 31 with other members of the UNSC (except Qatar) for **Resolution 1696**, demanding that Iran suspend nuclear enrichment; calling upon countries to prevent technology transfers to Iran's nuclear enrichment and missile programs; requesting an IAEA report on Iran's compliance by August 31; and warning of sanctions if Iran does not comply. After negotiations over Russian and PRC objections to the first U.S. and European draft resolution on sanctions, China voted with all other Security Council members for **Resolution 1737** on December 23, 2006, which invoked Article 41 of Chapter VII to require Iran to suspend nuclear enrichment and reprocessing activities, and heavy water-related projects. On January 5, 2007, in Beijing, PRC President Hu Jintao stressed the "unanimous" adoption of Resolution 1737 to visiting Iranian nuclear official Ali Larijani. After negotiations on additional sanctions on Iran (during which China and Russia objected to a ban on Iran's arms imports and export credit guarantees for doing business in Iran),[28] China voted with all other members of the UNSC for **Resolution 1747**, adopted unanimously on March 24, 2007. Citing Article 41 of Chapter VII, the resolution banned Iran's arms exports.

However, the United States raised the problem with China of its violation of UNSC Resolutions 1737 and 1747. In particular, U.S. officials reportedly said in July 2007 that earlier in the year, a PRC "entity" (probably one under U.S. sanctions) tried to ship a large amount of chemicals used to make solid fuel for ballistic missiles. Cooperating with U.S. intelligence, Singapore intercepted the container from China on its way to the Shahid Bagheri Industrial Group in Iran.[29] This Iranian organization was listed in the Annex of UNSC Resolution 1737, but sanctions for entities or people in the Annex involved restricting travel and freezing financial assets. Still, Resolution 1737 decided that all States take the necessary measures to prevent transfers directly or indirectly from their territories that could contribute to Iran's development of nuclear weapon delivery systems. Resolution 1747 called for restraint in transfers related to arms and missiles to Iran.

After the IAEA reported on May 23, 2007, that Iran continued nuclear enrichment activities, the Bush Administration called for a third UNSC resolution with tougher sanctions on Iran.[30] On September 28, China joined with the United States, France, Germany, Russia, and United Kingdom in issuing a foreign ministers' statement in support of negotiations, the IAEA, as well as a third UNSC resolution with sanctions. However, on October 17, China refused to attend a meeting in Berlin on Iran's nuclear program, citing "technical" difficulties. China apparently tried to make a linkage to an unrelated matter. U.S. officials said China showed displeasure over that day's award in the U.S. Capitol of the Congressional Gold Medal to Tibet's Dalai Lama.

---

[28] "Nations Closer to Deal on Iran Sanctions," *AP*, March 13, 2007; and Colum Lynch, "6 Powers Agree on Sanctions for Iran," *Washington Post*, March 16, 2007.

[29] Jim Wolf, "U.S. Faults China on Shipments to Iran," *Reuters*, July 12, 2007; Neil King Jr., "China-Iran Trade Surge Vexes U.S.," *Wall Street Journal*, July 27, 2007.

[30] Karen DeYoung, "Iranian Defiance of U.N. Detailed," *Washington Post*, May 24, 2007; State Department, Daily Press Briefing, July 26, 2007.

Even as the UNSC expected the IAEA's report and PRC Foreign Minister Yang Jiechi visited Tehran on November 13, China's Foreign Ministry spokesman criticized sanctions as being of "no help." Two days later, Under Secretary of State Nicholas Burns expressed concerns about China's increasing civilian and military trade with Iran and called on China to agree to have the next meeting on sanctions and "take a much more resolute role."[31] China again did not attend a meeting scheduled for Brussels on November 19, citing "scheduling reasons."

On December 3, 2007, the United States issued a new National Intelligence Estimate (NIE) on Iran's nuclear capabilities, finding that, in the fall of 2003, Iran had halted its nuclear *weapons* program but in January 2006, resumed its declared uranium enrichment activities. In response, the PRC's ambassador at the U.N. claimed that the situation for imposing more sanctions changed. (Later, in the Section 721 Report to Congress for 2009, U.S. intelligence reported an assessment that Iran kept open the option to develop nuclear weapons without knowing whether Iran eventually will decide to produce nuclear weapons. Also, Iran continued uranium enrichment.)

Nonetheless, in January 2008, China's shifted to support a third sanctions resolution at the UNSC, upon talks with Deputy Secretary of State John Negroponte who visited China for the bilateral Senior Dialogue and argued for another UNSC resolution because of Iran's violation of the previously passed resolutions. Foreign Minister Yang Jiechi attended a six-nation meeting on sanctions at Berlin on January 22, 2008. However, Yang reportedly agreed to a draft UNSC resolution only with compromise language that excluded new sanctions on freezing the assets of Iranian banks and military units, and on Iran's arms imports.

Based on the compromise in January, the U.N. Security Council passed (with Indonesia abstaining) **Resolution 1803** on March 3, 2008. This third UNSC sanctions resolution called for travel restrictions and bans; bans on dual-use nuclear trade; "vigilance" in export credits and financial transactions with Iranian banks; and cargo inspections. At the same time, China stressed that the sanctions would not affect its "normal" business with Iran and called for negotiations.

While the United States and other countries sought a fourth set of UNSC sanctions on Iran, top PRC leader Hu Jintao met with Iranian President Mahmoud Ahmadinejad in Beijing on September 6, 2008, and expressed respect for Iran's right to peaceful use of nuclear energy as well as support for the nuclear non-proliferation regime. China raised another concern when it tried to link the six-nation diplomacy on Iran's nuclear program to U.S. arms sales to Taiwan. After the Bush Administration notified Congress on October 3 of proposed arms sales to Taiwan, the PRC blocked U.S. efforts to set up a conference call among the six countries to discuss Iran.[32] But later, on February 4, 2009, PRC Assistant Foreign Minister Liu Jieyi showed up at a six-nation (E3+3) meeting in Wiesbaden, Germany, to discuss Iran's nuclear program.

In April 2009, the **Obama Administration** shifted policy to participate regularly in E3+3 talks with Iran. At the same time, some observers in the EU reported that "because of a lack of any real leverage over China on the issue [of Iran's nuclear program], other than pointing to the threat of U.S. or Israeli attack on Iranian nuclear sites, the EU has been unable to persuade China to back tougher sanctions." They also pointed out that China actually shielded Iran from tougher sanctions and reinforced its economic influence in Iran.[33]

---

[31] Quoted by Robin Wright, "U.S. to Seek New Sanctions Against Iran," *Washington Post*, November 16, 2007.

[32] Matthew Lee, "China Blocks New Iran Sanctions Talks," *Associated Press*, October 16, 2008; Author's consultation.

[33] John Fox and Francois Godement, "A Power Audit of EU-China Relations," European Council on Foreign Relations, (continued...)

The Obama Administration also sought to "reset" the relationship with Russia for closer cooperation, which seemed to increase the isolation of China on the issue of whether to apply greater multilateral pressure on Iran. After Iran disclosed to the IAEA in September 2009 what was a second, secret uranium enrichment plant at Qom, Russia proposed that Iran send enriched uranium to Russia for processing for use in a research reactor. Russian President Dmitry Medvedev also discussed possible sanctions. (In 1995, Russia and Iran signed a contract for a Russian-built nuclear reactor at Bushehr in Iran. In 2005, Russia proposed that Iran transfer nuclear material from the Russian-built nuclear plant to Russia and to conduct nuclear enrichment at a facility in Russia. On November 16, 2009, Russia's Energy Minister indicated that the reactor would not start operations in 2009 due to "technical" reasons, but the announcement came one day after Presidents Barack Obama and Medvedev expressed concerns in a meeting in Singapore about Iran's uranium enrichment program.)[34] In February 2010, Russia joined France and the United States in criticizing Iran when it announced a plan to enrich uranium to 20% U-235, developments that further increased pressure on the PRC to sanction Iran.

A week after President Obama's summit in Beijing on November 17, 2009, at which he pressed China to cooperate in dealing with Iran, PRC Foreign Minister Yang Jiechi called Secretary of State Hillary Clinton. Prior to the summit, Administration officials had traveled to Beijing to warn that Israel regarded Iran's nuclear program an "existential" threat and could bomb Iran. The PRC told Clinton of its support for an **IAEA resolution** critical of Iran. The IAEA passed a resolution on November 27, censuring Iran's nuclear enrichment facility at Qom. Further, in February, April, and October 2010, Israel sent officials to China to urge its cooperation to sanction Iran. As discussed above, the Administration urged Saudi Arabia and the UAE to increase oil supplies to China to reduce its dependence on Iran's oil. Moreover, visiting the two countries in March 2010 for talks that included sanctions against Iran, Defense Secretary Robert Gates confirmed that all the Persian Gulf states were worried about Iran's nuclear program and missile proliferation, and he asked the Saudi king to urge China to support UNSC sanctions against Iran.[35]

Thus, China faced increased international pressures to act on additional sanctions against Iran. Still, in diplomatic negotiations on another UNSC Resolution for a fourth set of sanctions, China reportedly opposed sanctions to target Iran's oil and gas industry. President Obama made some progress with PRC leader Hu Jintao when he attended the Nuclear Security Summit in Washington on April 12, 2010, and Hu used the word "sanctions" for work at the UNSC.[36]

On June 9, 2010, China voted for **UNSC Resolution 1929** to impose sanctions against Iran. The resolution simply noted the potential connection between Iran's revenues derived from its energy sector and funding of Iran's nuclear activities. Among the sanctions, the resolution called on all countries to prevent the direct or indirect supply to Iran of certain major weapons. Later, in testimony to the House Foreign Affairs Committee on March 1, 2011, Secretary of State Clinton confirmed to Congress that China "went along" with the UNSC sanctions on Iran only "after much diplomatic effort and arm twisting."

(...continued)

April 2009.

[34] *AP*, November 18, 2005; *Financial Times*, September 25, 2009; *New York Times*, October 1, 2009.

[35] *Washington Post*, November 26, 2009; IAEA Resolution Gov/2009/82, November 27, 2009; *Jerusalem Post*, February 28, 2010; *American Forces Press Service*, March 11, 2010; *Sunday Times*, April 4, 2010; *New York Times*, June 8, 2010; *Jerusalem Post*, October 7, 2010.

[36] *Guardian*; *Washington Post*; *Associated Press*, April 14, 2010.

As the United States and other nations imposed unilateral sanctions including ones that targeted Iran's energy sector, concerns increased that China could fill in gaps and exploit such sanctions (as discussed above). Days before Hu Jintao's state visit in Washington on January 19, 2011, the United States and EU discouraged China from joining Iran's invited tour of its nuclear sites, rather than IAEA inspections, and China implied that it declined to visit. Days later, on January 22, China was said to stay in solidarity with others in P5+1 talks with Iran.[37] The **U.S.-PRC Joint Statement** issued at that summit called for full implementation of UNSC Resolutions on Iran, but it did not refer to the other sanctions or oppose Iran's nuclear activities. Indeed, the statement noted positively Iran's right to peaceful uses of nuclear energy under the NPT. Moreover, State Department official Robert Einhorn in March criticized China for its mixed implementation of UNSC sanctions on Iran and said that Iran was suspected of getting nuclear-related items in China. Earlier the same month, Malaysia seized suspected cargo on a ship from China bound for Iran. Meanwhile, the U.N. also investigated Iran's attempt to acquire phosphor bronze from a company in China, though China cooperated in the seizure of the banned material in South Korea. Further, from October 2008 to January 2011, the manager of a company in China helped a citizen of Iran to procure U.S. materials that could be used in gas centrifuges to enrich uranium.[38]

On November 8, 2011, the IAEA reported in GOV/2011/65 about "possible military dimensions" to Iran's nuclear program and development of a "nuclear explosive device." The IAEA warned that, since 2002, it "has become increasingly concerned about the possible existence in Iran of undisclosed nuclear related activities involving military related organizations, including activities related to the development of a nuclear payload for a missile." With Russian resistance as cover, China urged the IAEA not to report the agency's evidence. Upon the release of the report, China responded that the IAEA should be "objective and just" and Iran should be flexible and sincere in "serious" cooperation with the IAEA. Though China voted on November 18 at the IAEA Board of Governors for a resolution of concern, it stopped short of reporting the matter to the UNSC.

Missile Technology Sales to Iran

Overview

During the Clinton Administration, PRC entities reportedly transferred equipment and technology to Iran's missile programs, including development of medium-range ballistic missiles. In November 2000, the Administration determined that PRC missile technology transfers took place but waived sanctions, citing a new PRC promise on missile nonproliferation. However, PRC entities reportedly continued missile-related proliferation activities in Iran. In contrast to the previous administration, the Bush Administration stressed the use of sanctions against PRC entities, including "serial proliferators."

---

[37] *Reuters*, January 5, 2011; PRC Foreign Ministry, January 13, 2011; *Washington Post*, January 22, 2011.

[38] *Bloomberg*, March 10, 2011; *The Star*, March 17, 2011; *Utusan*, March 18, 2011; *Reuters*, March 22, 2011; Department of Justice, "Two Indicted for Alleged Efforts to Supply Iran with U.S. Materials for Gas Centrifuges to Enrich Uranium" (statement on indictment of Parviz Khaki, arrested, and Yi Zongcheng, remained at large), July 13, 2012; Joby Warrick, "Nuclear Ruse: Posing as Toymaker, Chinese Merchant Allegedly Sought U.S. Technology for Iran," *Washington Post*, August 12, 2012.

Obama Administration

The Obama Administration has continued to impose sanctions. This record raised questions about the effectiveness of sanctions as well as the PRC's commitment and capability to control exports to Iran. (See **Table 1** on sanctions.) In February and April 2009 and July 2010, the United States imposed sanctions on PRC entities and Li Fangwei for missile proliferation in Iran. The United States subsequently imposed repeated sanctions on such entities or individuals. Also, in July 2009, the State Department reportedly had concerns that Q.C. Chen (a PRC person previously sanctioned for weapons proliferation) arranged for the sale of a test chamber to Iran's Defense Industries Organization that could be useful for testing missile parts. The test chamber was made by Voetsch China (a PRC subsidiary of a German firm) and was not controlled by the MTCR.[39] In February 2011, the Section 721 Report for 2011 told Congress that PRC "entities" continued to supply missile-related items to Iran. The report also said that entities in the PRC (and Russia and North Korea) likely supplied key components for Iran's production of ballistic missiles.

North Korea's Missile and Nuclear Weapons Programs

Suspected Missile Supplies

Since 1998, there have been public reports about and U.S. government confirmation of PRC assistance to North Korea's missile program. There were questions about whether the PRC had interests in North Korea's missile advances. Lieutenant General Xiong Guangkai, a Deputy Chief of General Staff of the People's Liberation Army (PLA), visited North Korea in early August 1998, before the surprising launch of a medium-range Taepo Dong-1 missile on August 31, 1998. However, increased worries about North Korea's missile program spurred U.S. and Japanese support for missile defenses opposed by China. Some said PRC entities acted on their own.

The National Security Agency (NSA) reportedly suspected in late 1998 that the China Academy of Launch Vehicle Technology (CALT) was working with North Korea on its space program (closely related to missiles) to develop satellites, but that cooperation was not confirmed to be linked to the Taepo Dong-1 MRBM program, the *Washington Times* reported (February 23, 1999). An NSA report dated March 8, 1999, suggested that China sold specialty steel for use in North Korea's missile program, reported the *Washington Times* (April 15, 1999). In June 1999, U.S. intelligence reportedly found that PRC entities transferred accelerometers, gyroscopes, and precision grinding machinery to North Korea, according to the *Washington Times* (July 20, 1999). An October 20, 1999, classified report said that China's Changda Corp. sought to buy Russian gyroscopes that were more of the same that China supplied to the North Korean missile program earlier that year, reported the *Washington Times* (November 19, 1999). In December 1999, the NSA discovered an alleged PRC deal to supply unspecified PRC-made missile-related items to North Korea through a Hong Kong company, said the *Washington Times* (January 1, 2000).

The DCI first publicly confirmed PRC supplies to North Korea, or Democratic People's Republic of Korea (DPRK), in July 1999. The DCI's April 2003 Section 721 Report said that, in the first half of 2002, North Korea continued to procure missile-related raw materials and components from foreign sources, but it dropped a previous reference about those foreign supplies as especially going through DPRK firms in China. There were direct implications for U.S. national

---

[39] "Inside the Ring," *Washington Times*, February 3, 2011.

security, because of North Korea's nuclear weapons and nuclear programs as well as delivery systems. PRC technology transfers have further implications for secondary, or retransferred, proliferation, since North Korea reportedly supplied technology to Iran, Syria, Pakistan, Egypt, Libya, and Yemen. The DNI's Section 721 Report of May 2007 told Congress that PRC "entities" continued in 2005 to assist North Korea's ballistic missile program.

There were indications that some sensitive exports from China continued to North Korea. Taiwan raided in July 2010 Ho Li Enterprises that received orders since March 2007 from Dandong Fang Lian Trading Company in Dandong, PRC, with an alleged association with the DPRK's military, for two dual-use, high-technology machine tools that ended up in North Korea earlier in 2010.[40] By early 2011, the DPRK reportedly built a new facility to launch long-range ballistic missiles, located close to China.[41] Further, the Section 721 Report for 2011 noted that the DPRK continued to procure missile-related materials and components from foreign sources. This ability still raised questions about China's control of trade at the PRC-DPRK border and compliance with UNSC resolutions that imposed sanctions on North Korea's missile and nuclear programs.

After the DPRK's failed launch of a Taepo Dong-2 missile on April 13, 2012, a military parade two days later in Pyongyang showed an apparent KN-08 ICBM on a 16-wheel transporter-erector-launcher (TEL) that reportedly originated from the PRC. The suspected PRC TEL raised concerns that included implications for threats to U.S. security, violations of UNSC sanctions, China's credibility as a UNSC Member that committed to and then undermined UNSC resolutions, U.S.-PRC cooperation, and whether U.S. sanctions would apply. Representative Michael Turner sent a letter on April 17 to Secretary of State Hillary Clinton and DNI James Clapper, asking about the suspected transfer of the TEL. At a hearing of the House Armed Services Committee two days later, Representative Turner asked Defense Secretary Leon Panetta, who testified that the DPRK's missile and nuclear capabilities posed threats and that the PRC provided help for the DPRK's missile program, though he did not specify the assistance. On April 19, the Foreign Ministry claimed that the PRC has implemented UNSC resolutions and PRC nonproliferation policies and export controls, and the State Department said at a news conference it took China at its word on the allegations. Still, in diplomatic channels, the State Department raised the alleged transfer with the PRC as a weapons proliferation concern. Meanwhile, an unnamed official of the Obama White House downplayed the PRC's help for the DPRK's missile program as "poor performance" in implementing sanctions (not "willful proliferation") and not a clear violation of UNSC sanctions, because the transfer supposedly entailed the chassis (not a complete TEL) and that could have been sold for "civilian" use by a DPRK front company.[42] The Obama Administration did not impose sanctions for the PRC transfer.

Nonetheless, the suspected WS51200 TEL in the DPRK was produced as a 122-ton vehicle by the Hubei Sanjiang Space Wanshan Special Vehicle Company, which is a part of the China Space Sanjiang Group under the China Aerospace Science and Industry Corporation (CASIC). They belong to the PRC's state-owned aerospace defense industry, producing products for the PLA. The Wuhan Sanjiang Import and Export Company shipped (on the *Harmony Wish*) four WS51200 vehicles from Shanghai to North Korea in August 2011, marking them on a shipping document as "off-road trucks."[43] Moreover, the PRC has controls at its border with the DPRK. Further, UNSC

---

[40] *Associated Press* and *Kyodo*, September 7, 2010.

[41] *Washington Post*, February 16, 2011.

[42] Mark Landler, "Suspected Sale by China Stirs Concern at White House," *New York Times*, April 20, 2012.

[43] *The Telegraph*, June 8; *Asahi Shimbun*, June 12; *Kyodo*, June 13; *Jane's Defense Weekly*, June 14, 2012.

Resolution 1695 of 2006 required all States to prevent transfers of missile and missile-related items, materials, goods, and technology to the DPRK's missile or WMD programs. Also adopted in 2006, UNSC Resolution 1718, *inter alia*, required all States to prevent the direct or indirect transfer to the DPRK of missiles, missile systems, or related materiel, determined by the UNSC or a special committee. UNSC Resolution 1874 of 2009 expanded that ban to cover all arms (except for small arms) and related materiel as well as financial transactions, technical training, advice, services, or assistance related to the provision, manufacture, maintenance, or use of such arms. Visiting Beijing on May 22, Special Representative for North Korea Policy Glyn Davies acknowledged to reporters that he raised the issue of how to reinforce UNSC-approved sanctions and take them seriously, though he insisted that the United States and China share interests of peace, stability, and denuclearization. Further, at the press briefing on June 13, the State Department confirmed concerns that PRC entities assisted the DPRK's missile program and the U.S. expectation that China enforce the U.N.'s sanctions. A U.N. panel found that many of the violations of sanctions involved China's entities, and China resisted releasing the report. Also, South Korea suspected that, in December 2012, China exported bauxite (aluminum ore), a material that could be used to manufacture missiles, to a weapons plant in North Korea.[44]

Secret Nuclear Programs

A serious case of secondary weapons proliferation involves North Korea's secret program to enrich uranium to develop nuclear weapons, a program that U.S. officials said was surprisingly acknowledged by North Korea to visiting Assistant Secretary of State James Kelly during talks in Pyongyang on October 4, 2002. This acknowledgment was not publicly disclosed by the Bush Administration until October 16, 2002, at a time when President Bush sought congressional authorization for the war against Iraq. By early 2007, however, U.S. officials restated the assessment of the highly enriched uranium (HEU) program.

The DCI's April 2003 Section 721 Report stated that the United States was suspicious of an uranium enrichment program in North Korea for "several years" but did not obtain "clear evidence indicating that North Korea had begun constructing a centrifuge facility until recently." While the DCI previously reported that North Korea has another program using plutonium that produced one or two nuclear weapons, the *Washington Post* reported on April 28, 2004, that U.S. intelligence newly estimated that North Korea had at least eight nuclear weapons.

DCI George Tenet testified to the Senate Intelligence Committee on February 24, 2004, that U.S. intelligence judged in the mid-1990s that North Korea had produced "one, possibly two, nuclear weapons" and the 8,000 fuel rods that North Korea claimed to have reprocessed into plutonium metal would provide enough plutonium for "several more." On February 16, 2005, the Director of the Defense Intelligence Agency, Vice Admiral Lowell Jacoby, testified that North Korea's Taepo Dong 2 intercontinental ballistic missile, which could have been ready for testing, "could deliver a nuclear warhead to parts of the United States in a two-stage variant and target all of North America with a three-stage variant." However, a test of that missile failed in July 2006.

This case raised a question about whether China's nuclear technology indirectly contributed to North Korea's nuclear weapons program through Pakistan, since China was the "principal supplier" to Pakistan's nuclear weapons program. There also were questions about whether China shared useful intelligence about its knowledge of any Pakistani-North Korean cooperation.

---

[44] *Asahi Japan Watch*, June 22, 2012; *TV Chosun*, January 13, 2013.

The *New York Times* and *Washington Post* reported on October 18, 2002, that U.S. officials believed Pakistan provided equipment, including gas centrifuges, for the North Korean uranium enrichment program, in return for North Korea's supply of Nodong MRBMs to Pakistan by 1998. The *Washington Post* added on November 13, 2002, that the Bush Administration had knowledge that Pakistan continued to provide nuclear technology to North Korea through the summer of 2002. Henry Sokolski of the Nonproliferation Policy Education Center wrote in *National Review Online* (November 19, 2002) that "one might call on Pakistan, Russia, and China to detail what nuclear technology and hardware they allowed North Korea to import."

The *New York Times* reported on January 4, 2004, about a history of nuclear technology proliferating from Pakistan's Khan Research Laboratories headed by Abdul Qadeer Khan and disclosed that he had transferred designs for uranium-enrichment centrifuges to China first. DCI George Tenet confirmed to the Senate Intelligence Committee on February 24, that North Korea pursued a "production-scale uranium enrichment program based on technology provided by A.Q. Khan." Particularly troubling was the reported intelligence finding in early 2004 that Khan sold Libya a nuclear bomb design that he received from China in the early 1980s (in return for giving China centrifuge technology), a design that China already tested in 1966 and developed as a compact nuclear bomb for delivery on a missile.[45] That finding raised an additional question of whether Khan also sold that bomb design to others, including Iran and North Korea.

Moreover, PRC firms could have been involved directly or indirectly in North Korea's nuclear weapons programs or weapons proliferation to other countries. In June 1999, authorities in India inspected the North Korean freighter *Kuwolsan* and found an assembly line for Scud ballistic missiles intended for Libya, including many parts and machines from China or Japan, according to the *Washington Post* (August 14, 2003). The *Washington Times* reported on December 9 and 17, 2002, that a PRC company in the northeastern coastal city of Dalian sold to North Korea 20 tons of tributyl phosphate (TBP), a dual-use chemical that U.S. intelligence reportedly believed would be used in the North Korean nuclear weapons program.

PRC Border, Ports, and Airspace

Questions have arisen about China's compliance with or enforcement of UNSC resolutions and even enabling of the DPRK's activities in allowing cross-border trade and transactions to and from North Korea as well as Pakistani, North Korean, and Iranian ships and planes to use PRC ports and airspace (and perhaps military airfields). China's possible cooperation in interdiction, restrictions in the use of its ports and airfields, law-enforcement, and intelligence-sharing has become a salient question in light of the Bush Administration's PSI announced in May 2003 (which China did not join). As part of the military trade between Pakistan and North Korea, in July 2002, Pakistan flew a C-130 transport aircraft to pick up missile parts in North Korea, reported the *New York Times* (November 24, 2002). In December 2002, the Spanish and U.S. navies interdicted a North Korean ship (*So San*) with Scud missiles bound for Yemen, and the Spanish Defense Minister reported that the ship's last port of call was in China. In addition, an Iranian ship stopped at the Tianjin port in China and picked up missile components before sailing on to North Korea to take delivery of missiles and rocket fuel in February and November 2002, reported the South Korean newspaper, *Joong Ang Ilbo* (December 19, 2002). From April to July

---

[45] Joby Warrick and Peter Slevin, "Libyan Arms Designs Traced Back to China," *Washington Post*, February 15, 2004; William Broad and David Sanger, "As Nuclear Secrets Emerge in Khan Inquiry, More Are Suspected," *New York Times*, December 26, 2004.

2003, China reportedly gave overflight rights to Iranian Il-76 cargo planes that flew to North Korea at least six times to pick up wooden crates suspected of containing cruise missiles, and the Bush Administration lodged a diplomatic protest with Beijing, reported *Time (Asian edition)* on July 14, 2003. At a hearing held by the Senate Foreign Relations Committee on September 11, 2003, on U.S.-China ties, Assistant Secretary of State James Kelly confirmed to Senator Russell Feingold that the State Department raised with China the problem of North Korean planes flying through PRC airspace or making refueling stops in China.

Then, in June 2005, China (and a Central Asian country) agreed to deny over-flight rights to an Iranian cargo plane that had landed in North Korea allegedly to pick up missile components. In November 2007, the Bush Administration reportedly raised concerns with China that an Iran Air plane was flying from North Korea via Beijing's airport to Iran with a shipment of missile jet vanes for Iran's missile program. In August 2008, India denied use of its airspace to a North Korean plane that stopped in Burma (Myanmar) and was scheduled to fly on to Iran with suspected cargo related to weapons proliferation.[46] Such incidents raised the question of whether China allowed overflight by planes from North Korea, had knowledge of their cargo, or shared intelligence with the U.N., United States, or other countries.

After North Korea's second nuclear test in May 2009 and the UNSC applied sanctions under Resolution 1874, the United Arab Emirates, in August 2009, seized a ship (*ANL Australia*) transporting North Korean weapons to Iran. However, after originating in North Korea, the cargo was first transferred in June to a PRC ship that docked at China's port cities of Dalian and Shanghai, where the cargo was then moved to the *ANL Australia*.[47] Then, in December 2009, a plane carrying weapons in contravention of U.N. sanctions headed from North Korea for Sri Lanka and other countries, with the North Korean weapons bound for Iran. Thailand's air force seized the Il-76 plane, when it landed in Bangkok to refuel. In November 2009, South Africa seized North Korea's weapons cargo bound for Congo, in violation of UNSC Resolution 1874, and the shipment was first loaded onto a ship docked in Dalian. China's port of Dalian, close to North Korea's port of Nampo, has been one of the critical transshipment points in China for North Korea's cargo.[48] China apparently has not seized such arms shipments.

On April 12, 2011, Senator Lugar introduced **S.Con.Res. 12**, which called for a presidential report on North Korean ships and planes that visited Burma via China. A report by a U.N. Panel of Experts, blocked at the UNSC by China in May 2011, found that Iran and the DPRK traded illicit missile technology using Air Koryo and Iran Air, involving transshipment through China. In May 2011, a monitored DPRK ship sailed near Shanghai to the South China Sea, possibly bound for Burma or Bangladesh with missiles and related parts, and turned around. In May 2012, South Korea seized sensitive graphite cylinders useable in a missile program that North Korea shipped on a PRC ship en route to Syria. In August, Japan seized five aluminum alloy rods (which could be used in nuclear centrifuges) from North Korea bound for Burma, among cargo on a Taiwan-owned ship that departed from Dalian, China. In late 2012, North Korea reportedly agreed to supply Scud missile parts to Egypt by air cargo through China, and missile technicians from the

---

[46] *New York Times*, October 24, 2005; Jay Solomon, Krishna Pokharel, and Peter Wonacott, "North Korean Plane Was Grounded at U.S. Request," *Wall Street Journal*, November 1, 2008; John Pomfret, "U.S. Asked China to Keep Missile Parts from Iran," *Washington Post*, November 29, 2010.

[47] *Financial Times*, August 28, 2009; *Yonhap*, September 10, 2009; *Washington Post*, December 3, 2009.

[48] *Reuters*, December 13, 2009; *Wall Street Journal*, December 22, 2009; *Yomiuri Shimbun*, January 10, 2010; *Reuters*, February 22, 2010 *AFP*, February 25, 2010; *Chosun Ilbo*, March 10, 2010; *Asahi Shimbun*, July 20, 2010.

China Precision Machinery Import-Export Corporation (CPMIEC) reportedly went to Egypt to work with North Korean technicians.[49]

PRC-DPRK Military Relationship

Questions have arisen about the PRC's military relationship with the DPRK, including any PLA contingency planning in the event of a crisis or collapse in North Korea and support for the DPRK regime (even as it attacked South Korea's naval ship and island in 2010). A related issue concerns the challenge in talking with the PLA about contingencies that also could involve the U.S. military and allies. Other key questions are about the PLA's knowledge of the DPRK's missile and nuclear programs, plans to secure weapons and nuclear material, willingness to share information with the United States and U.S. allies, and aim to exert control that could complicate U.S. and Republic of Korea (ROK) operations. The PLA has called the DPRK a "buffer," keeping U.S. and ROK forces below the 38th parallel. Concerning operations at sea, PLA General Ma Xiaotian, in July 2010, expressed "opposition" to even U.S.-ROK exercises in the Yellow Sea.

As discussed in this report, the PRC and DPRK militaries had high-level contact just before the missile tests of August 1998 and July 2006. Moreover, this relationship has raised questions about China's effectiveness in using leverage with the power-holders in Pyongyang. When asked on October 14, 2009, whether the United States and China discussed contingencies in North Korea, Assistant Secretary of State Kurt Campbell acknowledged talks about "every" aspect. However, in February 2010, a professor at Peking University and a close observer of PRC policies warned that Beijing would not accept an implosion in Pyongyang or watch passively if other countries gain political and military control in North Korea. The professor later wrote in March 2012 that while Beijing seeks denuclearization, some PRC leaders actually hold the United States, rather than the DPRK, more responsible for tensions on the Korean peninsula.[50]

Indeed, China seemed to have shifted from pressuring North Korea with the military relationship to propping up the DPRK regime's security and survival. In August 2003, *Wen Wei Po* (a PRC-owned newspaper in Hong Kong) printed an article questioning whether the PRC-North Korean alliance under the 1961 Treaty of Friendship, Cooperation, and Mutual Assistance continued to serve China's interest. China took steps that appeared to pressure North Korea, including using the PLA. In September 2003, China replaced paramilitary People's Armed Police (PAP) troops with PLA soldiers along its border with North Korea, as confirmed by the PRC Foreign Ministry and the official *People's Daily* (September 16, 2003), apparently to warn North Korea against provocations. Reports appeared in 2006 to confirm the PLA's construction of fences along the border, although that construction reportedly had started in 2003. The Defense Department reported to Congress in 2004 with a skeptical critique that China "avoided taking real steps to pressure North Korea." Nonetheless, the report confirmed that "as a potential hedge against uncertainty, the PLA assumed responsibility for border security along the northeast frontier in fall

---

[49] *Telegraph*, May 12; *Reuters*, May 14; *New York Times*, May 14; *Kyodo*, May 17; *Reuters*, May 18, 2011; *Wall Street Journal*, June 14, 2011; *Reuters* and *Korea Times*, November 14, 2012; PRC Foreign Ministry, November 14, 2012; State Department's statement, November 15, 2012; *Asahi Japan Watch*, November 24, 2012; *Wall Street Journal*, November 28, 2012; *Free Beacon*, December 13, 2012, and January 29, 2013; *AFP*, March 18, 2013.

[50] Wang Jisi as quoted in *Korea Herald*, Seoul, February 24, 2010; Kenneth Lieberthal and Wang Jisi, "Addressing U.S.-China Strategic Distrust," Brookings Institution, March 30, 2012.

2003, increasing security along the porous border with North Korea and strengthening China's ability to stem refugee flows or respond to a breakdown of the North Korean regime."[51]

At the same time, China pursued military contacts with the United States (including Secretary of Defense Donald Rumsfeld's visit to Beijing in October 2005), even while China's traditional military friendship with North Korea showed greater candor. When PRC ruler Hu Jintao visited Pyongyang in October 2005 and Kim Jong Il visited China in January 2006, PRC media downplayed Hu's third position as Chairman of the Central Military Commission (CMC) (in addition to other positions as Communist Party General-Secretary and PRC President). On March 9, 2006, General B.B. Bell, Commander of U.S. Forces Korea, testified to the House Armed Services Committee that PRC-North Korean military engagement was "quite low" and that despite the friendship treaty, "the amount of military support that the PRC provides to the North is minimal." The PLA hosted the visit in May 2006 of Admiral William Fallon, Commander of the Pacific Command, to the Shenyang Military Region (close to the border with North Korea).

PRC Defense Minister and CMC Vice Chairman Cao Gangchuan visited North Korea in April 2006 for three days. But he did not get an audience with Kim Jong Il, raised the controversy of the DPRK's nuclear program, and then visited South Korea for five days in the same month. Just months after General Cao's visit, Pyongyang tested a Taepo Dong-2 missile in July 2006 and a nuclear device in October 2006. When the top PLA officer and another CMC Vice Chairman, General Guo Boxiong, visited Washington in July 2006, he criticized North Korea's July 4 missile test, even citing the UNSC's Resolution that condemned the test. Further indicating strains, on the day after the DPRK's nuclear test on October 9, 2006, the PRC Foreign Ministry publicly said that the test had a "negative impact" on PRC-DPRK ties and denied that China was North Korea's "ally." A PRC-owned newspaper in Hong Kong reported that PLA and PAP troops were on high alert at the PRC-DPRK border.[52] On October 16, the PLA commemorated the death of a soldier who was killed by North Korean soldiers a year earlier.[53]

However, following Pyongyang's second nuclear test in May 2009, PRC Defense Minister Liang Guanglie visited North Korea for five days on November 22-27. General Liang reportedly recalled that he was a veteran of the Korean War in which PRC-DPRK friendship was "sealed in blood." He met with Kim Jong Il but did not mention North Korea's nuclear program or denuclearization, in contrast to reporting of Defense Minister Cao's visit in 2006.

After South Korea announced on May 20, 2010, an international finding that North Korea attacked South Korea's naval ship, *Cheonan*, on March 26, killing 46 sailors, CMC Vice Chairman Guo Boxiong visited the Shenyang Military Region apparently in early June, including its troops at the border with North Korea. In July, the PLA also "opposed" U.S.-ROK maritime exercises in the whole Yellow Sea, seemingly supporting the DPRK which was the target of the exercises to enhance deterrence and defense. In August, the PRC Executive Vice Minister of Public Security Liu Jing visited North Korea to hold talks and donate equipment to the Ministry of People's Security which was identified as under the National Defense Commission. At a higher level, PRC Minister of Public Security Meng Jianzhu visited Pyongyang on February 13-14, 2011, arriving two days after protestors in Egypt ousted President Hosni Mubarak. Minister Meng signed an agreement to cooperate with the DPRK, before he got a meeting with Kim Jong Il. In

---

[51] Defense Department, "Report on PRC Military Power," May 29, 2004.

[52] *Wen Wei Po*, October 13, 2006.

[53] *South China Morning Post*, October 17, 2006.

April, the DPRK allegedly launched a cyberattack that was staged from China against South Korea, in the first public report of a cyberattack by one country against another's bank. In July, the PRC gave or sold 3,000-4,000 military trucks and jeeps to North Korea. The next month, PRC Defense Minister, General Liang Guanglie, met with a DPRK military officer on logistics.[54]

In November 2011, Kim Jong Il and Kim Jong Un received PLA General Li Jinai, a CMC Member who conveyed greetings from Hu Jintao as Party leader but not CMC Chairman. Just after the PLA's visit, the DPRK announced on November 30 that it made progress in uranium enrichment. However, after Kim Jong Il died, Hu Jintao on December 20 expressed condolences also as the CMC Chairman, in a rare invocation of this military title in dealing with North Korea. Hu promptly expressed support for Kim Jong Un, even before he was named as Supreme Leader. In mid-2012, the PLA and civilian forces held exercises at the Yalu River and elsewhere near the DPRK (including in a counter-terrorism scenario), but with no reported DPRK participation. During PRC Defense Minister Chang Wanquan's visit to Washington in August 2013, the PLA's Director of Foreign Affairs spoke to selected reporters and called for the U.S. side to be "flexible" toward North Korea and spoke against sanctions to deal with its nuclear weapons program. The next month, however, Under Secretary of Defense for Policy James Miller called on the PRC to maintain and increase pressure on North Korea to achieve denuclearization.

Trilateral and Six-Party Talks in Beijing

Overview and PRC Policy

After the Bush Administration's October 2002 disclosure about North Korea's ongoing nuclear weapons programs, it sought a multilateral effort (not just bilateral negotiations) to achieve the complete, verifiable, and irreversible dismantlement (CVID) (not just a freeze) of North Korea's nuclear weapons programs (uranium and plutonium programs) as well as nuclear weapons. The Administration's strategy relied on securing China's cooperation and central role. At the October 25, 2002, summit in Crawford, TX, top PRC ruler Jiang Zemin agreed with President Bush on the goal of a nuclear-free Korean peninsula achieved through a peaceful resolution, although Jiang claimed to be "completely in the dark" about North Korea's nuclear weapons.

However, some have raised issues of whether China has been helpful in fully using its leverage with North Korea, whether it seeks North Korea's denuclearization with as much urgency as the United States and its allies, whether China's role warrants a closer U.S.-PRC relationship that risks other U.S. interests, and whether China actually undermines regional stability, given its support for the status quo that includes a provocative, belligerent DPRK. China has balanced its own various concerns that include (1) sustainment of a "friendly" U.S. approach toward China; (2) U.S. security policies (suspected of provoking instability and collapse of a fellow Communist regime, with loss of a perceived "buffer" between PLA and U.S. forces); (3) diminished global standing in any appearances of isolated PRC influence; (4) Beijing's losses and wins with Washington, including any limits to U.S. arms sales to Taiwan; (5) U.S. alliances with Japan and South Korea; (6) a stronger Japan (with missile defense and even possibly nuclear weapons); (7) stability and PRC influence on a weak North Korea; (8) a strong, unified Korea; and (9) sustaining a fellow Communist regime and legacies of past leaders to preserve power.

---

[54] *Chosun Ilbo*, August 23, 2011; *Xinhua*, August 26, 2011; *Washington Post*, August 30, 2011.

China commonly has cited a concern about "stability" (e.g., jeopardized by DPRK refugees). However, China's view appears different from that of the United States and others. In response to Kim Jong Il's death in December 2011, PRC Foreign Minister Yang Jiechi called for "peace and stability," but Secretary of State Clinton's statement did not use "stability." Some have suspected the PRC's preference for the status quo, even though that involves the DPRK's provocations of instability and repression. Beijing's cited concern was belied by the continuation into 2012 of smuggling of drugs and people plus other illicit activity across the PRC-DPRK border and more relaxed military patrols and other controls on China's side of the border. Also, the PRC acknowledged in February that it repeatedly repatriated certain DPRK citizens over 10 times.[55]

Initially, China did not respond to multilateral cooperation with the urgency and to the extent sought by the United States. Then, North Korea further escalated the situation by expelling IAEA inspectors and reactivating its nuclear reactor at Yongbyon in December 2002, and by withdrawing from the NPT in January 2003. On February 7, 2003, Bush said he had to "remind" Jiang of "joint responsibilities" in achieving "common" objectives concerning North Korea. Two days later, Secretary of State Colin Powell said in an interview on *Fox News Sunday* that China had "considerable influence with North Korea." Powell reported that North Korea depended on China for 80% of its energy and economic activity, and urged China to play an active role in the dispute. Later, in November, Powell said that after he had pressed the need for China to "rise to its responsibilities in dealing with this regional problem," PRC Vice Premier Qian Qichen made an "important contribution" in March 2003 by delivering the message in North Korea that "there would be no alternative to multilateral talks" that involved China and other countries.[56]

Starting in 2003, as North Korea further exacerbated the security situation, China's stance shifted to sponsor multilateral talks to denuclearize the Korean peninsula, to be openly critical of North Korea, and to support tough UNSC resolutions that condemned the July 2006 missile firings and that imposed sanctions for the October 2006 nuclear test by the DPRK. However, the PRC also urged the United States to provide aid to North Korea, to lift sanctions, to hold bilateral U.S.-DPRK talks by 2007 (even outside of Beijing), and to show flexibility for a final settlement. While skeptics pointed to progress as limited to the *process* of the Beijing-sponsored talks, there appeared some initial progress in *results* by the summer of 2007, with the shutdown of North Korea's Yongbyon nuclear reactor. Nonetheless, in spite of the PRC's role in sponsoring negotiations with and supporting North Korea, its "isolated" position in multilateral negotiations, and the seeming fragility of the health of the North Korean ruler and economy, the North Korean regime retained time to stall denuclearization, diplomatic leverage, economic gains, repression of its people, ways for weapons proliferation, and a capability for additional nuclear tests.

Trilateral Talks (April 2003)

After the PRC's pressure on North Korea in March 2003, China hosted Trilateral Talks among China, the DPRK, and the United States on April 23-25, 2003. Secretary Powell noted positively that "China has stepped up." However, the DCI's Section 721 Report (of November 2004) confirmed that, at the meeting, North Korea threatened to "transfer" or "demonstrate" its nuclear weapons. On June 9, 2003, in Tokyo, Deputy Secretary of State Richard Armitage "saluted" China's cooperation on North Korea and declared "a new phase of our relationship with China."

---

[55] *Jane's Intelligence Review*, January 27, 2012; PRC Foreign Ministry, press conference, February 28, 2012.

[56] Department of State, "Secretary of State Colin L. Powell's Remarks at Conference on China-U.S. Relations," College Station, Texas, November 5, 2003.

1ˢᵗ *Round of Six-Party Talks (August 2003)*

Responding to U.S. insistence on expanded multilateral talks, China hosted the first round of the Six-Party Talks (also including South Korea, Japan, and Russia) on August 27-29, 2003. However, North Korea again threatened to transfer or test a nuclear weapon, as confirmed by the DCI's Section 721 Report of November 2004. Then, China seized a shipment of tributyl phosphate (TBP), a material used for nuclear weapons, suspected by the CIA on a train bound for North Korea in the summer of 2003, reported *Asahi Shimbun* (February 22, 2004). The DCI's Section 721 Report confirmed that, in September 2003, at the border with North Korea, China stopped a shipment of chemicals that could have been used in the DPRK's nuclear program.

2ⁿᵈ *Round (February 2004)*

The Bush Administration sought another round of multilateral talks before the end of 2003, with a tentative date set by November for around December 17,[57] but the talks were not held then. When PRC Premier Wen Jiabao visited President Bush at the White House on December 9, 2003, the Taiwan question eclipsed the issue of North Korea. The *Washington Post* disclosed on January 7, 2004, that at a meeting in Seoul the week before, a PRC diplomat, Fu Ying, questioned the credibility of U.S. intelligence that Pyongyang had a highly enriched uranium program.

China then hosted the second round of Six-Party Talks on February 25-28, 2004, for which Assistant Secretary of State James Kelly expressed appreciation. However, North Korea denied the suspected uranium enrichment program. The State Department's statement after the talks did not report any progress in either freezing or dismantling North Korea's nuclear weapons programs, but pointed to "progress on a regularized process" for peacefully resolving this issue.

3ʳᵈ *Round (June 2004)*

Before China hosted another round of Six-Party Talks, PRC Deputy Foreign Minister Zhou Wenzhong publicly questioned the credibility of U.S. intelligence about North Korea's uranium enrichment and expressed support for North Korea's arguments (in an interview with the *New York Times*, June 9, 2004). China hosted the third round of talks on June 23-26, 2004. The DPRK again threatened to test a nuclear weapon. Afterward, National Security Adviser Condoleezza Rice traveled to Beijing and told CMC Chairman Jiang Zemin and President Hu Jintao that "A.Q. Khan was not engaged in academic research" and that "North Korea has a highly enriched uranium program," reported the *Washington Times* on July 14, 2004.

Despite the lack of any breakthrough in the Trilateral Talks and three rounds of Six-Party Talks held since April 2003, Assistant Secretary of State James Kelly contended at a hearing of the Senate Foreign Relations Committee in July 2004 that multilateral diplomacy was useful and that the talks held in Beijing yielded progress in dealing with the threat of North Korean nuclear weapons.[58] In answer to Senator Chuck Hagel, Kelly acknowledged that "there could be and probably should be a role for the United Nations Security Council (UNSC)," but reported that China likely will not be interested in dealing with the threat at the UNSC. In answer to Senator

---

[57] *Kyodo News*, November 24, 2003.

[58] Senate Foreign Relations Committee, hearing, *A Report on Latest Round of Six-Way Talks Regarding Nuclear Weapons in North Korea,* July 15, 2004.

Lincoln Chaffee, Kelly denied that China linked cooperation on North Korea to U.S. concessions on Taiwan (including arms sales), by saying that China did not pose Taiwan "as a tactical issue" in discussions about North Korea. Kelly acknowledged to Senator Bill Nelson that it remained unclear as to whether China's preference for positive incentives (over pressure) will work.

In early February 2005, President Bush sent Michael Green, the National Security Council's Senior Director for Asian Affairs to Beijing, Tokyo, and Seoul to intensify diplomatic pressure on Pyongyang. In Beijing, Green met with President Hu Jintao and reportedly presented urgent U.S. intelligence findings that North Korea had processed several tons of uranium hexafluoride (which could be enriched to make nuclear bombs) and sold some to Libya perhaps in early 2003.[59] Other reports, however, pointed to intelligence findings that the material originated in North Korea but that Pakistan bought the uranium hexafluoride and supplied it to Libya.[60]

Suspension of Six-Party Talks

On February 10, 2005, North Korea again escalated tensions by announcing that it would indefinitely suspend its participation in the Six-Party Talks and that it had manufactured nuclear weapons. North Korea's announcement further called into question China's preference for positive inducements and raised the issue of using sanctions to pressure Pyongyang, including consideration of action by the UNSC. Instead of using China's economic and other leverage on North Korea, the Foreign Ministry contended at a news conference on February 17 that sanctions would only complicate the situation (a position that Foreign Minister Li Zhaoxing argued to Secretary of State Rice on February 12). China instead urged U.S.-North Korean bilateral talks.

The Bush Administration then stepped up pressure on the PRC to use its leverage to bring North Korea back to the talks. On March 21, 2005, Secretary of State Rice met with top PRC officials including President Hu in Beijing, after visiting other Asian capitals. She urged China in particular to help restart the Six-Party Talks, publicly saying that "China has the closest relationship with North Korea," that "it is not a U.S.-North Korean issue," and that "there are other options in the international system."[61] In Beijing on April 26, 2005, Assistant Secretary of State Chris Hill reportedly raised the idea of an interruption of oil flows from China to North Korea, but China refused.[62] On April 28, President Bush reminded China about his agreement with Jiang Zemin and mentioned Secretary Rice's option of going to the U.N. Security Council (where China has veto power). A PRC Foreign Ministry official publicly blamed Washington for a "lack of cooperation" and Bush for calling Kim Jong Il a "tyrant" at a news conference.[63] At a congressional hearing on May 26, Hill said that China had "enough influence" to convince North Korea to return to the talks but had not done it. He also made China accountable for any failure of the Six-Party Talks if it failed to get its "very close friend" back to the talks.[64]

---

[59] David Sanger and William Broad, "Tests Said to Tie Deal on Uranium to North Korea" and "U.S. Asking China to Press North Korea to End its Nuclear Program," *New York Times*, February 2 and 9, 2005.

[60] Glenn Kessler and Dafna Linzer, "Nuclear Evidence Could Point to Pakistan," *Washington Post*, February 3, 2005; Dafna Linzer, "U.S. Misled Allies About Nuclear Export," *Washington Post*, March 20, 2005.

[61] Secretary Condoleezza Rice, "Remarks to the Press in China," Beijing, March 21, 2005.

[62] Glenn Kessler, "China Rejected U.S. Suggestion to Cut Off Oil to Pressure North Korea, *Washington Post*, May 7, 2005.

[63] Joseph Kahn, "China Says U.S. Impeded North Korea Arms Talks," *New York Times*, May 13, 2005.

[64] House International Relations Subcommittee on Asia and the Pacific, hearing on Northeast Asia, May 26, 2005.

Meanwhile, Secretary Rice also offered a strengthened U.S.-PRC relationship and agreed that Deputy Secretary of State Robert Zoellick would hold the first "Senior Dialogue" with his PRC counterpart, a meeting which was scheduled for early August 2005. PRC ruler Hu Jintao had requested what China called "strategic talks" when he met with President Bush in November 2004.[65] One day after North Korea announced on July 9 that it would return to the talks, Secretary Rice visited China, but this time before visiting U.S. allies (Thailand, Japan, and South Korea).[66]

4th Round and Joint Statement (July-September 2005)

After a period of 13 months without talks, China announced the start of the fourth round of the Six-Party Talks in Beijing on July 26, 2005, and described China's role as both a "host" to "facilitate" the talks and a "participant." The inconclusive first phase of this round ended on August 7, when the countries agreed to recess and resume talks on August 29. Pakistani President Pervez Musharraf provided support for U.S. reports of North Korea's uranium enrichment program, when he said that A.Q. Khan supplied North Korea with centrifuges and their designs.[67] North Korea did not return to the talks as agreed but returned later on September 13. Meanwhile, President Bush agreed to meet at the White House with Hu Jintao in early September but had to postpone because of Hurricane Katrina. Bush then met with Hu in New York on September 13.

China proposed a joint statement that recognized North Korea's insistence on a light water reactor and had no explicit mention of a uranium program. On September 17, PRC Vice Foreign Minister Dai Bingguo presented China's draft as the "most realistic" and put pressure on the United States to agree to it.[68] Along with other countries, the United States agreed to sign the **Joint Statement of Principles (not an agreement) on September 19, 2005**, in which North Korea committed to abandon "all nuclear weapons" and "existing nuclear programs" and to return to the NPT and IAEA safeguards; and the other countries agreed "to discuss, at an appropriate time, the subject of the provision of a light water reactor." However, the United States had to clarify separately that dismantlement of nuclear weapons must be verifiable; that nuclear programs included plutonium and uranium; and that an "appropriate time" for "discussion" of a light water reactor would be when North Korea has verifiably eliminated all nuclear weapons and all nuclear programs.[69]

At a hearing of the House International Relations Committee on October 6, 2005, Representative Ileana Ros-Lehtinen asked about PRC pressure to accept the deal. Assistant Secretary of State Chris Hill did not deny that Beijing exerted pressure and noted that there were earlier PRC drafts that were "absolutely unacceptable," while the mention of a light water reactor was "not welcomed." He testified, nonetheless, that the United States benefitted from China's strong desire to reach a deal and that "we can work well with the Chinese." He also described China's role as that of a "secretariat" (producing drafts), seemingly a neutral role.

---

[65] Department of State, Daily Press Briefing, April 8, 2005; Deputy Secretary of State Robert Zoellick, "Remarks at U.S. Embassy Beijing," August 2, 2005; and Glenn Kessler, "Zoellick Details Discussions With China on Future of the Korean Peninsula," *Washington Post*, September 7, 2005.

[66] Secretary Condoleezza Rice, Press Availability in Beijing, July 10, 2005.

[67]*BBC*, August 24, 2005; and *New York Times*, September 13, 2005.

[68] *Xinhua [New China News Agency]*, September 17, 2005; and Joseph Khan and David Sanger, "U.S.-Korean Deal On Arms Leaves Key Points Open," *New York Times*, September 20, 2005.

[69] Department of State, "Joint Statement of the Fourth Round of the Six-Party Talks," Beijing, and "North Korea—U.S. Statement," New York City, September 19, 2005.

5*th* *Round (November 2005)*

After the joint statement of September 2005 was signed, PRC Vice Premier Wu Yi traveled to North Korea on October 8-11, 2005, promising new economic aid. Top PRC leader Hu Jintao then followed with a visit on October 28-30 and attended a ceremony to sign economic agreements. On November 1, China announced that the next round would start on November 9. While there was progress in the *process*, when the meeting for the 5th round of the Six-Party Talks ended on November 11, no progress in *results* was announced for the implementation of the joint statement to dismantle North Korea's nuclear weapons. Moreover, there continued to be differences between the U.S. and PRC approaches in continuing the Six-Party Talks. While President Bush called for "firm resolve" in a speech given in Kyoto, Japan, on November 16, 2005, the PRC's Hu Jintao called for "greater flexibility" in a speech in Seoul the next day.

PRC Communist Party General-Secretary Hu Jintao hosted North Korean ruler Kim Jong Il in China on January 10-18, 2006, and Hu expressed support for the Six-Party Talks. The PRC proposed a meeting on January 18 in Beijing between Assistant Secretary of State Chris Hill and North Korean negotiator Kim Kye-gwan. China's media said that PRC diplomat Wu Dawei "also joined" the implied U.S.-DPRK bilateral meeting (vs. the U.S. view of a three-nation meeting).

On February 3, 2006, Senators Harry Reid (Democratic Leader), Carl Levin (Ranking Democrat of the Armed Services Committee), Joseph Biden (Ranking Democrat of the Foreign Relations Committee), and John Rockefeller (Vice Chairman of the Intelligence Committee) wrote a letter to President Bush, saying that U.S. policy "still has not resulted in an elimination, freeze, or even a slowing of North Korea's nuclear and ballistic missile activities." At a hearing of the House International Relations Subcommittee on Asia and the Pacific on March 8, 2006, Chairman James Leach critiqued President Bush's "reactive" approach to the Six-Party Talks that "appear moribund," calling for U.S. leadership, "initiative" for more dialogue, "greater flexibility" for diplomacy, sending Assistant Secretary of State Chris Hill (the witness) to Pyongyang, negotiation of a permanent peace on the peninsula at a separate forum, direct contacts with North Korean officials, and liaison offices to solve a "problem of communication." Leach argued against continuing to "transfer the initiative to others, indebting us to the diplomacy of countries that may have different interests or simply ensconcing the status quo."

Indeed, despite its considerable influence, China's balanced role placed its stance as more neutral than supportive of the United States and its allies. Moreover, while Beijing pursued the "process" of the talks, results remained elusive. The burden increased on China's preferred diplomacy to achieve the DPRK's nuclear disarmament. The impasse also threatened to strain U.S.-PRC ties.

Missile Tests (July 2006)

The impasse continued into the summer of 2006, when China failed to prevent North Korea from test-firing seven ballistic missiles, including the first test of a Taepo Dong-2 ICBM under development with a range (perhaps 3,700 miles) that could reach Alaska.[70] After the DPRK began preparations in May, Congress expressed concerns, including in a letter from Senators Carl Levin and Hillary Clinton to President Bush on June 15. At a hearing of the House Armed Services

---

[70] In a radio interview on July 8, 2006, Secretary of Defense Donald Rumsfeld said that North Korea announced it has nuclear weapons and ballistic missiles, but it is uncertain whether North Korea has the ability to mate a nuclear weapon with a ballistic missile. Also, he said that North Korea has 3-5 more "Taepodong-2 airframes."

Committee on June 22, some Members asked about China's role. Brigadier General John Allen, the Pentagon's Principal Director for Asian and Pacific Affairs, testified that the PRC tried to dissuade North Korea from steps that would be destabilizing and undermine the Six-Party Talks. However, the PRC's use of leverage, including the PLA's opposition or acquiescence to the DPRK's missile program, was unclear. Indeed, there was high-level military contact between the PRC and DPRK shortly before the July 2006 missile tests, similar to that before the August 1998 missile firing. On June 21, 2006, the PLA Chief of General Staff, General Liang Guanglie, told a DPRK military visitor that the PLA will "expand cooperation" with the Korean People's Army.

On July 4, 2006 (Washington time), North Korea provocatively fired a Taepo Dong-2 ICBM that failed in less than 40 seconds after launch and several short-range Scuds and medium-range Nodongs. On July 5, Senator John McCain stated that China and Russia have the most leverage over North Korea and warned that their postures would have a heavy impact on our relations.

In a phone call with President Bush on July 6, PRC ruler Hu Jintao expressed "deep concerns" about the "situation" but also warned against actions that might "aggravate the situation."[71] On July 7, with U.S. support, Japan sponsored a UNSC resolution that invoked Chapter VII of the U.N. Charter (language for sanctions and/or force), but China countered with a non-binding statement by the UNSC president with no mention of Chapter VII. China's draft statement of July 10 called for resuming the Six-Party Talks, preventing technology and financial transfers to North Korea's missile and WMD programs, and other voluntary measures. Tokyo and Washington agreed on July 10 to postpone a vote on their resolution to give time for Beijing's diplomacy.

China sent a scheduled delegation led by Vice Premier Hui Liangyu to Pyongyang on July 10-15 to commemorate the 45th anniversary of the bilateral friendship treaty, and Hui reportedly signed a new agreement on economic aid. But Kim Jong Il snubbed the PRC visitor. Although China was given time for this mission, Beijing intensified its criticism of Tokyo on July 11, calling its resolution an "overreaction." Assistant Secretary of State Chris Hill reported from Beijing on July 12 that China's delegation failed to achieve progress in getting Pyongyang back to the talks.

On July 12, China (and Russia) reportedly dropped their pursuit of a draft statement to sponsor a draft UNSC resolution that countered Japan's resolution primarily by withholding authority under Chapter VII (for sanctions or use of force). Still, China's resolution called for nations to resume the Six-Party Talks and refrain from supplying technology or funds to the DPRK's missile program. Despite similar goals, Beijing's envoy threatened to veto Tokyo's resolution.

Ultimately, negotiations led to **UNSC Resolution 1695** that was adopted unanimously on July 15, 2006, condemning the DPRK's missile launches, demanding that it suspend its missile program, requiring all countries to prevent technology transfers to its missile or WMD programs, requiring countries to prevent missile proliferation from the DPRK and financial transfers to its missile or WMD programs, as well as urging the DPRK in particular to show restraint and return to the Six-Party Talks (with implementation of the September 2005 Joint Statement and abandonment of all nuclear weapons and nuclear programs). While in St. Petersburg, Russia, for the Group of Eight summit, President Bush thanked Hu Jintao for his "leadership" on the resolution. Also, on July 26, 2006, the White House confirmed reports that in late 2005, China had frozen North Korean assets at the Bank of China for counterfeiting the PRC currency.[72]

---

[71] The official *China Daily*, July 7, 2006.

[72] *Yonhap News*, July 24, 2006; *Reuters* and *Zhongguo Tongxun She*, July 26, 2006.

Nonetheless, at a hearing of the Senate Foreign Relations Committee on July 20, 2006, Chairman Richard Lugar pointed out that China facilitated talks on the DPRK while continuing to supply key energy and lifelines into North Korea. He warned that although China wanted to avoid regional instability, the missiles tests were destabilizing; China's ability to secure global benefits for its high economic growth rates depended on continued cooperation with the West; and "Beijing must reassess its regional priorities." It remained unclear whether China supported use of Chapter VII, although Assistant Secretary Hill testified that the resolution's language on "international peace and security" was a reference to Chapter VII. Despite the UNSC resolution, China criticized Japan's sanctions on September 19 and refused to attend a meeting of eight countries to discuss the DPRK at the U.N. two days later.

In September 2006, the House and Senate passed the conference report for the FY2007 NDAA (**P.L. 109-364**), which required the President to appoint a **North Korea Policy Coordinator** to review policy and report to Congress. The Administration did not comply with an appointment. Congress later repealed the requirement in the FY2008 NDAA (**P.L. 110-181**).

First Nuclear Test (October 2006)

On October 3, 2006, North Korea warned that it would conduct a nuclear test, and China reacted the next day by singling out North Korea to use restraint. On October 9, North Korea conducted a nuclear test. On the same day, even as President Bush reacted with no confirmation of the test, China confidently expressed its "opposition" to North Korea for "flagrantly" conducting a nuclear test. The next day, a PRC-owned newspaper in Hong Kong specifically reported that North Korea conducted a nuclear test 300 meters underground with an explosion of 800 tons.[73] China's strongly negative reaction to this nuclear test reflected a heighten fear of instability on its periphery and frustration at North Korea's defiance of China's leaders. (On October 16, 2006, the Director of National Intelligence publicly confirmed this nuclear test of "less than a kiloton." President Bush issued a formal determination on December 7, 2006, declaring that North Korea detonated a nuclear explosive device on October 9, 2006.)

The PRC Foreign Ministry urged resuming the Six-Party Talks. China also agreed to UNSC sanctions but opposed using force or the PSI, which China did not join.[74] The United States and Japan compromised with China and Russia, which urged "balance" (targeted arms embargo, no ban on ships and aircraft, restrictive language for "measures under Article 41" (sanctions) of Chapter VII, and "cooperative" action including cargo "inspections" to prevent proliferation).

On October 14, 2006, China voted with all other members of the UNSC for **Resolution 1718**, imposing sanctions to prevent the supply of major weapons as well as items that could contribute to the DPRK's nuclear, missile, or other WMD programs; luxury goods; transfers of funds for those programs; travel by people responsible for those programs; and inspection of cargo to prevent WMD proliferation. Secretary Rice praised China for its "remarkable evolution." On October 17, Rice left for Japan and South Korea (allies first), China, and Russia, saying she

---

[73] *Ta Kung Pao*, October 10, 2006.

[74] China likely has concerns about any military action by Japan, including logistical support for U.S. naval ships conducting inspection and interdiction at sea. Also, China became highly sensitive to U.S. inspection or interdiction at sea in 1993, when China was the target of U.S. inspection of a cargo ship called Yinhe, which was suspected of supplying chemicals to Iran. See CRS Report 96-767, *Chinese Proliferation of Weapons of Mass Destruction: Background and Analysis*, by Shirley A. Kan.

expected every country to "fully implement all aspects" of Resolution 1718. She defended the Administration's approach, saying "what the President has done in putting together this coalition, with China at the center of it willing to go along with Chapter 7, is quite remarkable."[75] In remarks in Beijing on October 20, Rice asserted that China was now committed to the DPRK's denuclearization, rather than Washington dealing bilaterally with Pyongyang.

However, China's enforcement of the resolution was questionable, as it called for "cooperative action" in "inspection" (and not interception or interdiction) of cargo. Also, while any PRC sanctions under its strict interpretation of Resolution 1718 might seek to counter the DPRK's weapons-related activities, they might not be sufficiently broad or effective in achieving the ultimate, unrealized goal of the dismantlement of North Korea's nuclear weapons and programs. China's agreement to ban luxury goods could have indicated its disapproval of the defiance of Kim's regime. However, "luxury goods" were not defined, and North Korean elites reportedly continued to enjoy shopping sprees across the border in Dandong, China.[76] Indeed, China increased the export of banned luxury goods to North Korea from 2006 to 2007.[77]

Immediately after voting for the resolution, the PRC ambassador stated his reservations that "China does not approve of the practice of inspecting cargo" to and from the DPRK. After imposition of sanctions, China's customs agents reportedly carried out more stringent inspections of cross-border traffic, perhaps to prevent dangerous transfers.[78] China seemed to have tightened "inspections" (to the letter of the resolution), without participation in military inspection or interdiction at sea. Also, after the nuclear test, China's major state-owned banks suspended financial transactions with North Korea and then relaxed restrictions around mid-November.[79]

Other than these initial and limited actions, PRC and foreign reports portrayed business as usual in PRC trade with North Korea.[80] The PRC Foreign Ministry also declared on October 17 that the "China-DPRK border is normal." China had numerous other options, including limiting its exports to and imports from North Korea, valued at $1.6 billion in 2005.[81] Limiting investments there and cracking down on smuggling were other PRC options. On October 22, PRC media reported the arrest of two people for smuggling uranium, possibly from North Korea, but that arrest took place in September 2006, before the nuclear test.[82] China also could have cut crude oil supplies (up to 90% of the DPRK's supplies). Some stoppage of supplies (in February 2005, February 2006, and September 2006) was reported, but that took place before the DPRK's nuclear test and not as sanctions. Also, PRC provision of diesel fuel as aid to North Korea continued. The amount of crude oil that the PRC exported to the DPRK remained the same in 2005 to 2007.[83]

---

[75] Secretary Condoleezza Rice, "Briefing on Upcoming Trip to Asia," October 16, 2006.

[76] Gordon Fairclough, "Close-out Sale: North Korea's Elite Shop While They Can," *WSJ*, December 18, 2006.

[77] Nicholas Kralev, "Chinese Exports Blunt U.N. Sanctions," *Washington Times*, December 19, 2008, citing a report by the Peterson Institute for International Economics.

[78] *AP*, October 16, 2006; *Yonhap*, October 17, 2006; *China Daily*, October 19, 2006.

[79] *JijiWeb*, Tokyo, October 25, 2006; a State Department official, November 13, 2006; *JijiWeb*, November 26, 2006; *Nihon Keizai Shimbun*, November 28, 2006. The PRC foreign ministry denied on October 24 that the PRC ordered the banks to stop "normal" commercial transactions with North Korea but did not deny the suspension of transactions.

[80] *Wen Wei Po*, October 17, 2006; *Huanqiu Shibao*, October 19, 2006; *New York Times*, October 27, 2006.

[81] *Zhongguo Jingying Bao*, October 16, 2006.

[82] *Liaoning Jingwang*, Shenyang, October 22, 2006; *Chosun Ilbo*, Seoul, October 24, 2006.

[83] *New York Times*, October 31, 2006; *Yonhap*, November 8, 2006; and Global Trade Atlas.

Continued 5th Round, Bilateral Meetings, and February 2007 Statement

On October 31, 2006, the PRC announced a trilateral meeting among PRC, DPRK, and U.S. officials in Beijing, at which they agreed to resume the Six-Party Talks "soon." Meeting reporters in the Oval Office, President Bush publicly thanked China for this bit of news. Nearly two months later, what China called the "second phase" of the fifth round took place in Beijing on December 18-22, 2006. China proposed "working groups"—including bilateral ones—and issued a statement citing "useful" talks on how to implement the September 2005 Joint Statement. However, Assistant Secretary Hill reported no breakthrough.

Significantly, on January 16-17, 2007, separately from the Six-Party Talks and for the first time outside of Beijing, Hill traveled to Berlin and held a bilateral meeting with his North Korean counterpart to make progress in the process of meetings. Hill indicated U.S. willingness and flexibility to use a "bilateral mechanism," with the specific approval of President Bush and Secretary Rice to resolve the problem.[84] Meanwhile in Beijing, Deputy Assistant Secretary of Treasury Daniel Glaser held separate talks with the North Koreans on sanctions that froze North Korean assets at a bank in Macau, the Banco Delta Asia (BDA). On January 30, 2007, Glaser resumed those talks in Beijing, and China said that the "third phase" would start on February 8.

On February 13, 2007, the six countries agreed to a **Joint Statement** based upon which North Korea would shut down the Yongbyon nuclear facility and allow IAEA inspections. The DPRK also would "discuss" with other parties a list of all nuclear programs that would be abandoned. The United States agreed to start bilateral talks with the goal of a diplomatic relationship and the removal of the DPRK from the list of state sponsors of terrorism. Five Working Groups were established: (1) denuclearization of the Korean Peninsula; (2) normalization of U.S.-DPRK relations; (3) normalization of DPRK-Japan relations; (4) economic and energy cooperation; and (5) Northeast Asian Peace and Security Mechanism. Based on the DPRK's progress in meeting the terms of the agreement, economic aid (including a total of 1 million tons of heavy fuel oil), a ministerial meeting including Secretary of State Rice, and negotiations for permanent peace on the Korean Peninsula were promised. Rice also said that the United States agreed to resolve, through a separate channel, the issue of whether to release North Korean funds at BDA.

Restated Assessment of Uranium Program

Shortly after the February 2007 Joint Statement, Assistant Secretary Hill updated the assessment of the DPRK's highly enriched uranium (HEU) program, saying that North Korea purchased some equipment (including Pakistani centrifuges from A.Q. Khan) and that there was a question of whether its procured aluminum tubes were used in a HEU program. Hill also said that "the North Koreans have not acknowledged having an HEU program."[85] Moreover, Joseph DeTrani, the DNI's Mission Manager for North Korea, testified on February 27 that whereas U.S. intelligence had "high confidence" in October 2002 that North Korea was acquiring material sufficient for a production-scale capability to enrich uranium, there was a change to "mid-confidence."[86] An unnamed U.S. official clarified in June 2007 that the 2002 finding of the

---

[84] State Department, Christopher Hill's briefing, Berlin, Germany, January 17, 2007.

[85] Christopher Hill, "Update on the Six-Party Talks," remarks to the Brookings Institution, Korea Economic Institute, and Asia Society, February 22, 2007.

[86] Senate Armed Services Committee, hearing on the "Annual Threat Assessment of the Director of National Intelligence," February 27, 2007.

DPRK's acquisition of equipment did not change, but confidence about the progress of the HEU program changed.[87] This re-statement could have given credence to the PRC's stated doubts about U.S. intelligence. The intelligence community (IC) told Congress in the Section 721 Report for 2007 that although North Korea halted and disabled portions of its *plutonium* production, "we assess with high confidence it has in the past pursued a uranium enrichment capability that we judge is for nuclear weapons and assess with at least moderate confidence that it continues to pursue such a capability." For 2008, the IC reported that "although North Korea has halted and disabled portions of its plutonium production program, we continue to assess North Korea has pursued a uranium enrichment capability at least in the past. Some in the IC have increasing concerns that North Korea has an ongoing covert uranium enrichment program."

6th Round and October 2007 Statement

The "sixth round" of talks began on March 19, 2007, and then adjourned on March 22, with North Korea demanding that its frozen funds (about $25 million) be released from BDA in Macau. After the Treasury Department worked with Russia to release the $25 million to North Korea on June 14, 2007, diplomacy resumed on the dismantlement of nuclear programs.

Again meeting bilaterally and not in Beijing, Assistant Secretary of State Hill visited Pyongyang on June 21 and briefed reporters in Washington four days later on U.S. goals for the disablement of the DPRK's Yongbyon nuclear reactor by the end of 2007 and "complete clarity" on the highly enriched uranium program. With the IAEA's verification, the DPRK shut down the reactor and related facilities at Yongbyon on July 14. The "Six-Party Talks" resumed on July 18-20. However, the Joint Statement issued by the PRC did not include a deadline for the DPRK's declaration of all nuclear programs and disablement of all nuclear facilities.

On September 1-2, 2007, Assistant Secretary Hill again held negotiations with North Korean officials outside of the Six-Party Talks in Beijing, this time in Geneva. He announced an agreement that the DPRK would provide a full declaration of all nuclear programs and disable nuclear programs by the end of 2007. Hill asserted that this was "not a bilateral process," but the PRC applauded the improved U.S.-DPRK relationship.[88]

Meanwhile, on September 16, China provided its first shipment of 50,000 tons of heavy oil to North Korea. When China hosted the "second session of the 6th round of the Six-Party Talks" on September 27-30 in Beijing, PRC Vice Foreign Minister Wu Dawei stressed the progress made by the Working Groups. Days later, China issued a **Joint Document on October 3, 2007**. In the statement, the DPRK agreed to disable all nuclear facilities, and this disablement focused on three facilities (including the Yongbyon reactor site) to be completed by December 31, 2007. The United States alone agreed to lead disablement work and provide funding. The DPRK also agreed to provide a "complete and correct declaration" of all nuclear programs. The DPRK reaffirmed its commitment on nuclear nonproliferation. The statement also discussed normalization of the U.S.-DPRK and Japan-DPRK relationships and a ministerial-level meeting with no set dates.

---

[87] Bill Gertz, "Data on N. Korea Centrifuges Sought," *Washington Times*, June 12, 2007.

[88] State Department, "North Korea to Disable Nuclear Programs by End of 2007," Geneva, Switzerland, September 2, 2007; "U.S.-DPRK Bilateral Working Group Talks End; DPRK Agrees to Declare its Nuclear Programs and Disable Its Nuclear Facilities," *China News Agency*, September 3, 2007; *Xinhua*, September 4 and 6, 2007.

Implementation and Impasse

However, the PRC-sponsored Joint Document of October 2007 raised a number of questions about implementation, including about the disposition of nuclear equipment (in North Korea, China, Russia, or elsewhere); disablement of nuclear facilities aside from the three cited; ultimate dismantlement of nuclear facilities; U.S.-only funding and work for disablement; declaration of nuclear weapons in addition to nuclear programs; clarification of uranium as well as plutonium programs; missile and nuclear proliferation (with the North Korean-built nuclear reactor in Syria just bombed by Israel in September);[89] nuclear testing sites; verification and monitoring; timelines for bilateral normalization; other concerns of the United States and Japan about human rights, terrorism, and abductions; strains in the U.S.-Japan alliance; coordination with Seoul; and the State Department's consultations with Congress, Defense Department, and European allies.

In November 2007, the Energy and State Departments assigned liaison officials in Pyongyang to monitor and pay for disablement at Yongbyon, including the unloading of reactor fuel rods. (U.S. officials said they worked productively until the DPRK regime kicked them out during the week of April 13, 2009.) Approaching the end of 2007 deadline for disablement and declaration, Assistant Secretary of State Hill went on his second visit to Pyongyang in early December 2007, bringing a letter from President Bush to Kim Jong Il. Upon the deadline of December 30, 2007, the State Department said it was "unfortunate" that North Korea failed to provide a complete and correct declaration of all nuclear programs and slowed down disablement work.

In early 2008, some critics contended that China failed to exert strong economic and diplomatic leverage with North Korea even as it claimed credit for hosting the talks. Former Under Secretary of State John Bolton wrote that "we are long past the point of allowing China to cover for Kim Jong Il without any cost in its relations with the U.S." Jay Lefkowitz, President Bush's Special Envoy on North Korean human rights, questioned the "misguided assumption" that China would apply significant pressure on North Korea to abandon nuclear weapons. He noted that the PRC's assistance to and trade with North Korea have "persisted with only brief interruptions."[90]

As the impasse continued into 2008, China's role came into greater question. China reportedly suspended food aid to North Korea at the start of 2008.[91] Hill and DPRK Vice Foreign Minister Kim Kye Gwan met bilaterally in Beijing on February 19 and in Geneva on March 13, 2008. In another meeting in Singapore in April, the United States and North Korea reached an compromise agreement (without a released text) that North Korea would declare its plutonium but separately "acknowledge" its uranium enrichment program and the nuclear reactor it built in Syria that Israel bombed the previous September.[92] On May 8 in Pyongyang, the DPRK provided to visiting U.S. State Department official, Sung Kim, documents related to plutonium production since 1986 at the Yongbyon facilities. The State Department continued to call for a complete and correct declaration from North Korea for outside verification.

---

[89] Barbara Opall-Rome and Vago Muradian, "Bush Privately Lauds Israeli Attack on Syria," *Defense News*, January 14, 2008; Paul Richter, "West Says N. Korea, Syria Had Nuclear Link," *Los Angeles Times*, January 17, 2008.

[90] John Bolton, "North Korea's True Colors," *Wall Street Journal*, January 11, 2008; and Jay Lefkowitz, U.S. Special Envoy for Human Rights in North Korea, "North Korean Human Rights and U.S. National Security," speech at AEI, January 17, 2008.

[91] *Hankyoreh*, Seoul, January 5, 2008.

[92] Glenn Kessler, "U.S. Ready to Ease Sanctions on N. Korea," *Washington Post*, April 11, 2008.

Partial Declaration and Verification Protocol

On June 17-19, 2008, PRC Vice President and Communist Party Politburo Standing Committee Member Xi Jinping visited Pyongyang and promised gifts or aid to the DPRK regime in the form of 5,000 tons of aviation fuel and about $15 million.[93]

Secretary Rice gave a speech on June 18, defending the "Six Party Talks" and reliance on China. She said, "our decision to support China as the chair of the six-party talks has also been a strong incentive for Beijing to conduct itself responsibly" on North Korea. She said that a goal is to formalize "these patterns of cooperation" into a Northeast Asian peace and security mechanism. She noted that the goal remained to verifiably eliminate "all of North Korea's nuclear weapons and programs." Rice stated that North Korea has proliferated nuclear technology to Syria and has pursued a uranium enrichment program, although the extent of those activities was unclear. She disclosed that there was troubling new information about North Korea's uranium enrichment capability. She said that after North Korea delivered its declaration of nuclear programs to China, President Bush would notify Congress of his intention to remove North Korea from the list of State Sponsors of Terrorism and to lift sanctions under the Trading with the Enemy Act. But she warned that "before those actions go into effect," the United States would assess North Korea's cooperation in verifying that nuclear declaration. Rice stressed, "we are insisting on verification." She called for rigorous verification as based on a detailed plan and involving the other five countries as well as the IAEA; on-site access to facilities; collection and removal of samples; forensic analysis of materials and equipment at North Korean sites and facilities; access to design documents and other records "for all facilities associated with production and processing of all nuclear materials in North Korea;" and interviews with North Koreans.[94]

A week after Xi Jinping's visit to Pyongyang, the DPRK complied with a partial declaration on its plutonium program. PRC Vice Foreign Minister Wu Dawei issued a statement on June 26, 2008, telling the DPRK to submit its declaration to China that day and the United States to remove the DPRK from the list of State Sponsors of Terrorism and from U.S. sanctions. Wu stated that there was agreement only on a "set of principles to guide the establishment of a verification regime."

On the same day, President Bush quickly complied with U.S. actions. He removed North Korea from sanctions under the Trading with the Enemy Act and notified Congress of his intention to rescind North Korea's designation as a State Sponsor of Terrorism to be possible in 45 days. Bush did not condition his actions on verification of the DPRK's nuclear programs, weapons, and proliferation, saying that "we will work through the six-party talks to develop a comprehensive and rigorous verification protocol." National Security Advisor Stephen Hadley acknowledged that he had not yet seen the declaration and that he was relying on a "process" to get a verification protocol in place within 45 days.[95] The next day, U.S. officials traveled to Yongbyon to see the destruction of the cooling tower of the reactor. The Administration agreed to pay $2.5 million for that televised explosion and to accept a concession for North Korean "acknowledgments" on uranium and proliferation. Bush agreed with PRC demands to keep the declaration secret.[96]

---

[93] *Yonhap*, Seoul, July 4, 2008; PRC Foreign Ministry news conference, Beijing, July 8, 2008.

[94] Secretary of State Condoleezza Rice, "U.S. Policy Toward Asia," speech at the Heritage Foundation, June 18, 2008.

[95] White House, "Statement by the Press Secretary on North Korea," "Memorandum for the Secretary of State," "President Bush Discusses North Korea," and "National Security Advisor Hadley Holds White House News Briefing on the North Korean Nuclear Declaration," June 26, 2008.

[96] Glenn Kessler, "Message to U.S. Preceded Nuclear Declaration by North Korea," *Washington Post*, July 2, 2008; (continued...)

Secretary of State Rice then traveled to Beijing at the end of June to praise China's "leading role" and to press for the need for a framework for verification and monitoring, acknowledging that "we moved some of the verification steps up into the second phase." (As discussed above, the Joint Document of October 2007 left a number of unsettled questions about implementation, including verification.) While Rice stressed the need to agree on verification and monitoring, PRC Foreign Minister Yang Jiechi did not mention this need in their public comments.[97]

For the first time since the previous September, the formal format of the Six-Party Talks resumed in Beijing on July 10-12, 2008, along with a bilateral U.S.-DPRK meeting in Beijing on July 8, to discuss the broad U.S. proposal for a verification protocol. The "Six-Party Talks" issued a press statement on agreeing to set up a verification framework, but that fell short of the U.S. requirements for rigorous verification, as Secretary Rice specified in June. There was no primary role for the IAEA and no mention of sampling, forensics, or schedules. Still, Rice allowed a ministerial meeting with her DPRK counterpart on July 23 at a regional meeting in Singapore. President Bush did not take the DPRK off the terrorism list when legally possible on August 11. North Korea announced on August 26 that it suspended disablement at Yongbyon on August 14.

Assistant Secretary of State Hill returned to Beijing in early September, contending that China understood the "urgency" and praising China's role in chairing the talks as "excellent," "active," "superb," and "crucial." He outlined the limited goal for the DPRK, "not asking for the declaration to be verified now," but "simply asking for the rules of how it will be verified." He acknowledged that the DPRK's declaration was not yet verifiable. Still, Hill also stated that after North Korea agreed on a verification protocol, then the United States would immediately remove North Korea from the list of State Sponsors of Terrorism. In the same month, National Security Advisor Hadley conceded that North Korea's nuclear declaration "was not the complete and correct declaration that we had hoped." Nonetheless, he stated that after the DPRK accepts the verification protocol, it would be taken off the terrorism list.[98] Instead, on September 22, the DPRK provocatively asked IAEA inspectors to remove surveillance cameras and seals at the reactor and then announced intention to resume nuclear reprocessing at Yongbyon.

Hill went back to Pyongyang on October 1-3, and afterwards, China applauded those bilateral negotiations. On October 11, 2008, in Washington, the United States announced a bilateral "agreement" with North Korea on "verification measures" that would include sampling and forensics and would be applied to plutonium, uranium, and proliferation programs. But there would not be a standard, primary role for the IAEA. The State Department issued a press statement and a fact sheet, but not the U.S.-DPRK "agreement" itself. The State Department vaguely cited agreement in a written joint document and "certain other understandings" for measures that "will serve as the baseline for a Verification Protocol."[99]

(...continued)

Bill Gertz, "Inside the Ring," *Washington Times*, July 24, 2008.

[97] Secretary of State Condoleezza Rice, "Remarks with Chinese Foreign Minister Yang" and "Remarks with the Press in Beijing," Beijing, June 29 and 30, 2008.

[98] Assistant Secretary of State Christopher Hill, "Evening Walkthrough at Six-Party Talks," September 6; "Press Briefing by National Security Advisor Stephen Hadley on Upcoming U.N. General Assembly," September 20, 2008.

[99] State Department, "U.S.-DPRK Agreement on Denuclearization Verification Measures," "Fact Sheet, U.S.-North Korea Understandings on Verification," "On the Record Briefing: Special Envoy for the Six-Party Talks Ambassador Sung Kim, Assistant Secretary of State for Public Affairs Sean McCormack, Assistant Secretary of State for Verification, Compliance, and Implementation Paula DeSutter, and Acting Assistant Secretary of State for International Security and Nonproliferation Patricia McNerney on North Korea," October 11, 2008.

However, despite the lack of a verification protocol, a timeline for one, or an agreement at the "Six-Party Talks," the Secretary of State "immediately" rescinded the designation of the DPRK as a State Sponsor of Terrorism. This controversial decision was a retreat from the earlier U.S. position of first getting DPRK acceptance of a verification protocol, as officials stated.

Even then, on November 12, 2008, the DPRK denied it had agreed to all the U.S. verification measures, specifically sampling, in the written agreement negotiated with Hill. After bilateral talks between Hill and his DPRK counterpart in Singapore on December 4-5, negotiators convened the "**Six-Party Talks**" in Beijing on December 8-11. They failed to get the DPRK's agreement on an effective verification protocol, despite the U.S.-DPRK "agreement" in October and what the United States called China's "crucial" role.

Missile and Nuclear Tests (April and May 2009)

After December 2008 and particularly after the DPRK's second nuclear test in May 2009, China's role has come under greater criticism. In a **U.S. policy debate**, critics charged that the "Six-Party Talks" saw their "final collapse," failed even to address the DPRK's nuclear weapons, and drove wedges into U.S. alliances with Japan and South Korea. In this view, during the Six-Party Talks, the DPRK continued to proliferate suspected nuclear technology to countries such as Syria and Burma. Moreover, successive U.S. administrations failed to keep North Korea free of nuclear weapons, while it advanced its ballistic missile and nuclear weapon programs. In contrast to U.S. compliments to China, some stressed that China failed to tighten aid to the North Korean military and party elite and that Beijing failed to use its leverage effectively on Pyongyang. Thus, the question in 2009 became how the United States should work with China while recognizing the problems if not failure in the Six-Party Talks. Some argued that the United States should recognize China as less critical, given its different priorities and support for the DPRK regime. In such a view, if the United States dealt directly and proactively with the DPRK, Washington could mitigate muddled or mixed messages controlled by Beijing in its own interests. The United States could center its approach on allies (not a Sino-centric approach) and enhance the role of Russia. In another view, the United States could continue to engage China given the DPRK's dependence on China and the U.S. goal of moving to broader resolution of tensions in Northeast Asia and contingencies in a crisis. Consistent with this consideration, a former Deputy Assistant Secretary of State focused on China in the second Bush Administration contended in 2011 that the PRC was constructive and "assertive" toward the DPRK between 2006 and 2008 and that the United States should promote a return of that PRC approach. Still, a strategic review by Henry Kissinger noted that the DPRK reversed two decades of negotiations with multilateral and bilateral efforts, while "process has overwhelmed substance." He added that "Pyongyang has used the negotiating forums available to it in a skillful campaign of procrastination, alternating leaps in technological progress with negotiating phases to consolidate it."[100]

---

[100] "Condi's Korean Failure," editorial, *Wall Street Journal*, December 16, 2008. Yoichi Kato, "Richard Armitage: Bush Administration Lacked Accountability," *Asahi Shimbun*, December 27, 2008. John Bolton, "Obama Promises Bush III on Iran," *Wall Street Journal*, January 2, 2009. Victor Cha called for urging China to tighten aid to North Korea in a PacNet article, "Bad Advice for Secretary Clinton," March 9, 2009. Dan Blumenthal and Robert Kagan, in "What to Do About North Korea," *Washington Post*, May 26, 2009, wrote that the proposition of looking to China for help has been discredited. But Michael McDevitt wrote in "North Korea as a Nuclear Weapons State," PacNet #41A, June 2, 2009, that the United States should start a serious discussion with China about all options in a strategic approach to North Korea, including regime change. Tom Christensen, "Advantages of an Assertive China: Responding to Beijing's Abrasive Diplomacy," *Foreign Affairs*, March/April 2011. Henry Kissinger, "North Korea Throws Down the Gauntlet," *New York Times*, June 4, 2009; and "The North Korean Fallout," *Washington Post*, August 9, 2009.

On January 23, 2009, the DPRK's Kim Jong Il met with Wang Jiarui, the visiting Director of the International Liaison Department of the Communist Party of China, and pledged to the "denuclearization of the Korean Peninsula" and praised China's role in the Six-Party Talks. On February 13, Secretary of State Hillary Clinton called the Six-Party Talks "a very important forum," indicating that President Obama would not reject the talks while seeking results. A week later, she appointed Stephen Bosworth as the Special Representative for North Korea Policy, but on a part-time basis. PRC Foreign Ministry official Wu Dawei quietly visited Pyongyang on February 17-19 on the eve of Clinton's visit to Beijing, but North Korea asked for light water reactors.[101] However, by early February, satellites detected that North Korea was preparing another test of its Taepodong-2 inter-continental ballistic missile (after a previous test in 2006).[102] North Korea claimed on February 23 that it would launch a "satellite," not test a missile.

Still, North Korea launched a **Taepodong-2 missile on April 5, 2009**, which passed over the Sea of Japan and the nation of Japan. According to the North American Aerospace Defense Command (NORAD), the missile's first stage fell into the Sea of Japan, and the other stages with the payload fell into the Pacific Ocean, but no object entered into orbit. The DPRK's missile appeared to have flown as far as 2,390 miles.[103] President Obama issued a statement that day, saying that the DPRK's launch of the Taepodong-2 missile was a clear violation of UNSC Resolution 1718 that prohibited North Korea from activities related to ballistic missiles, and he called for action by the UNSC. The U.S. position saw such activities as covering the similar space launch vehicles and did not see a "satellite launch" as allowed in a loophole. PRC official media published a rare interview with a specialist of the PLA's Second Artillery (missile force) who stressed that missile and satellite launches involved similar technologies, except for a warhead.[104] In the end, on April 11, China agreed to a compromise to condemn the launch as a violation of Resolution 1718 but with a **UNSC Presidential Statement** rather than a resolution as preferred by the United States and Japan.[105] On April 13, the UNSC issued a presidential statement that condemned the launch, with no mention of any "satellite," and called for designating targets of sanctions under 1718. China's enforcement of such sanctions again raised a concern.

On April 13, the DPRK regime responded by kicking out U.S. Departments of Energy and State officials and IAEA inspectors, and re-starting nuclear facilities. Then, the DPRK regime conducted a **second nuclear test on May 25, 2009**, Memorial Day in the United States. (The Director of National Intelligence (DNI) issued a statement on June 15 that North Korea probably conducted an underground nuclear explosion on May 25, 2009, that yielded a few kilotons. The DNI's Section 721 Report for 2009 assessed progress in the DPRK's nuclear program, reporting to Congress that the nuclear test in 2009 was apparently more successful than the test in 2006. On February 16, 2011, the DNI testified to the Senate Select Committee on Intelligence that the United States did not know whether the DPRK produced nuclear weapons, despite the tests.)

On the day of the nuclear test, the UNSC issued a **Presidential Statement** to condemn the nuclear test as a violation of Resolution 1718. The United States, South Korea, and Japan agreed to seek a new UNSC resolution with sanctions. In addition, South Korea announced that it finally

---

[101] *JoonAng Daily*, February 27, 2009; *Kyodo*, March 19, 2009.

[102] Jay Solomon and Siobhan Gorman, "U.S. Believes North Korea May Be Preparing Long-range Missile Test," *Wall Street Journal*, February 3, 2009.

[103] Craig Covault, "North Korean Rocket flew Further Than Earlier Thought," *Spaceflight Now*, April 10, 2009.

[104] *Qingnian Cankao*, Beijing, April 7, 2009.

[105] Colum Lynch, "Key U.N. Powers Agree on N. Korea Statement," *Washington Post*, April 12, 2009.

joined the U.S.-led PSI, a step that could convince China that the situation in the Korean peninsula was destabilizing and to take stronger steps against North Korea. (On June 26, 2009, Representative Ros-Lehtinen introduced **H.Res. 604** in part to congratulate South Korea for joining PSI and to urge China and other nations not in PSI to implement UNSC resolutions. Later, in October 2010, South Korea hosted a multinational PSI drill for the first time.)

On May 30, 2009, even the PLA's lower-level representative to the Asian defense ministers' conference (Shangri-la dialogue) in Singapore, Deputy Chief of General Staff Ma Xiaotian, criticized North Korea's second nuclear test. But that was not the first time that a senior PLA officer criticized North Korea's provocations. As discussed above, the top PLA officer, General Guo Boxiong, visited Washington in July 2006 and criticized North Korea's July 4 missile tests.

The question was whether China would change its calculation about the situation in North Korea, shift its approach, and work more effectively to change the DPRK's behavior. In late May and June 2009, PRC policy analysts and academics in civilian and military domains in Beijing engaged in a **heated debate** about North Korea and whether its actions threatened China's interests, even to include whether China should abandon the special friendship that has protected the DPRK as a "buffer" for China. In a much-cited survey reported in an official newspaper, 10 academics favored severe sanctions on North Korea, while 10 opposed such abandonment of North Korea. The newspaper also published highly critical commentaries, including one suggesting that China would have to deal with the problem of the DPRK regime.[106] China was most concerned with the addition of more nuclear powers on its periphery, with North Korea and possibly Japan and South Korea (rather than another U.S. concern, that of North Korea's proliferation of nuclear technology to rogue regimes and terrorists). However, while there was academic anger in Beijing, official observers remained conservative and some pointed to the United States instead of reflecting on China's ambivalent approach. The PRC seemed to value retaining its unique central role and elevated importance in U.S. policy. Despite North Korea's defiance in seeking nuclear power status, there remained uncertainty about a major change in PRC policy including whether it would implement sanctions under existing or new UNSC resolutions. Reportedly, PRC policymakers reviewed their approach toward North Korea.

On June 5, 2009, Deputy Secretary of State James Steinberg met in Beijing with State Councilor Dai Bingguo and other officials to discuss the response at the UNSC and the broader Northeast Asian situation, before concluding his visits that took him also to Singapore, Tokyo, and Seoul, and flying back to Washington that night. However, Foreign Minister Yang Jiechi told Steinberg that there would be no major change in PRC policy, according to official PRC media.

Five days later, China agreed with other countries at the UNSC on new sanctions in a draft resolution. Then, on June 12, 2009, the UNSC approved **Resolution 1874** to expand the sanctions previously imposed under Resolution 1718 in 2006. This time, the sanctions banned all of the DPRK's arms exports but banned only some arms imports, with exclusion of small arms and light weapons (reportedly because China insisted on the right to sell arms to North Korea). Resolution 1874 called for denial of services for and inspections of ships suspected of carrying banned cargo, but excluded the use of force and required consent of the flag state for inspections on the high seas. It called for denying financial support and services that could contribute to the DPRK's

---

[106] Author's consultations in Beijing; also Tang Xiang, "Many Noted Chinese Scholars Support More Severe Sanctions to be Imposed on DPRK," *Huanqiu Shibao [Global Times]*, May 26, 2009; Sun Zhe, "DPRK Conducts Nuclear Blackmail," *Huanqiu Shibao*, May 26, 2009; Zhu Feng, "China Must Defend the Authority of the Six-Party Talks," *Huanqiu Shibao*, June 4, 2009; Zhu Feng, "North Korea Nuclear Test and Cornered China," PacNet #41, June 1, 2009.

proliferation activities and prohibited programs. It called on countries to implement the previous Resolution 1718. China expressed opposition to the DPRK's nuclear test but also opposition to use of force and called for restraint and resumption of the Six-Party Talks.

However, concerns increased not only about China's **enforcement of sanctions** but also whether it could benefit by expanding its economic interests as other countries reduced ties to North Korea. Only on April 24, 2009, did the UNSC list three North Korean entities subject to sanctions imposed under 1718. Then on July 16, 2009, the UNSC designated some entities, goods, and individuals sanctioned under Resolution 1718. On August 3, China submitted a required report to the UNSC on its implementation of the sanctions under Resolutions 1718 and 1874, promising generally to implement controls according to the UNSC's lists of items embargoed for export to the DPRK, to freeze assets of listed individuals or entities, and to deny entry into China of listed people. However, the PRC did not report specific steps, promised only to "refrain" from exporting weapons to the DPRK (excepting small arms and light weapons while these could be used domestically in the DPRK), did not include a ban on exporting luxury goods to the DPRK, and stood against sanctions that affect the DPRK's "national development," "lives," or "normal" international ties. In spite of Resolution 1718's sanctions announced in 2006 on luxury goods, the UNSC did not issue a list of such banned goods imported by the DPRK's elite.[107]

In addition to the previous questions about China's enforcement of that ban on **luxury goods** for North Korea, an unnamed PRC company tried to complete an order made in February 2009 by an Austrian firm for two yachts suspected of going to Kim Jong Il instead of China as claimed. Italy blocked the $18 million contract in July 2009.[108] Meanwhile, in June, Japan arrested a South Korean resident for exporting in October and December 2008 34 pianos and four Mercedes-Benz cars (the cars that North Korean diplomats and other elites have used for decades) from Japan to the Rungra Trading Company in Pyongyang (also called Room 39 to benefit Kim Jong Il) through the Dalian Global Company in Dalian, China. In July 2009, the Department of the Treasury had information that the China Guangfa Bank engaged in business with the DPRK's arms dealer, Global Trading and Technology (a front for Korea Mining Development Trading Corporation).[109] Also, in December 2009, Japan arrested two traders who exported expensive cosmetics from Japan to North Korea in October 2008, again through Dalian Global. In addition, about 100 cars, called F3 and made by BYD in China, crossed the border to North Korea through Dalian in April 2010.[110] (On November 4, 2010, the United States imposed sanctions on the DPRK regime's Green Pine Associated Corporation, Reconnaissance General Bureau, and Office 39.) China's port city of Dalian has been named as a major trans-shipment point for the DPRK regime.

Concerning **maritime interdiction**, in June 2009, just after the UNSC passed Resolution 1874 to sanction North Korea after its second nuclear test on May 25, the U.S. Navy's USS *John McCain* tracked a North Korean ship (*Kang Nam 1*) as it sailed toward Burma. Surprisingly, Burma then told North Korea that the ship would not be allowed to dock if it carried weapons or banned materials, and the ship returned to North Korea. Meeting at the Defense Consultative Talks in Beijing on June 24, Under Secretary of Defense Michele Flournoy said that she and the PLA did not discuss enforcement of the resolution against the ship off China's coast, claiming the meeting

---

[107] On December 5, 2011, the UNSC issued Implementation Assistance Notice No. 3: Guidelines for the Implementation of Measures Regarding "Luxury Goods" Contained in Security Council Resolutions 1718 and 1874.

[108] *Financial Times*, July 22, 2009; *Associated Press*, July 23, 2009.

[109] *South China Morning Post*, September 10, 2011.

[110] *Kyodo*, June 9, 2009, December 1, 2009; *Sankei Shimbun*, February 3, 2010; *TV Asahi*, April 14, 2010.

was not "appropriate" to discuss such "operational" details.[111] But at the ASEAN Regional Forum (ARF), Secretary of State Hillary Clinton said on July 23 that the United States asked China and Southeast Asian countries to convey to Burma concerns about the North Korean ship. She also confirmed concerns about military, including nuclear, cooperation between North Korea and Burma. (Back in November 2005, Senator Richard Lugar wrote of concerns about their military cooperation to the State Department.) Clinton praised China for "full implementation" of 1874.

In July, China released information through a local newspaper that Customs agents confiscated a rare metal used to produce alloy steel (called vanadium) being smuggled to North Korea. In the same month, China's NHI Shenyang Mining Machinery Company suspended construction of a bronze mine in North Korea with a company subject to U.N. sanctions. In August, the DPRK's Korea Kwangson Banking Corporation, under U.S. sanctions, closed in Dandong, China.[112] After the DPRK's nuclear test in October 2006, there were also reports of China's initial actions.

On October 4, PRC Premier Wen Jiabao visited Pyongyang and signed bilateral agreements to provide economic and technical assistance. Then the day after, Kim Jong Il reportedly told Wen that North Korea would attend multilateral talks that include "Six-Party Talks," but depending upon U.S.-DPRK talks on "peaceful" ties. Assistant Secretary of State Kurt Campbell promptly visited Beijing on October 14 and praised U.S.-PRC coordination as "tight and close," reminiscent of his predecessor Chris Hill's praise in 2008. U.S. coordinator of sanctions Philip Goldberg visited Beijing on October 20 and called on China to implement sanctions.

Thus, despite a debate, the PRC leadership apparently decided against a fundamental change in policy toward North Korea in part because of an assessment that its nuclear program presented no direct threat to China; that it instead posed a challenge to U.S. interests; that Beijing could buy time for stability; and that Beijing perceived no strong U.S. pressure to help on a top priority.[113] Critics have suspected China's preference for a *process* to talk, bolster its role, and sustain the status quo (that includes a divided Korean peninsula), in contrast to the United States and allies, particularly South Korea and Japan, that seek real *results* in the stated goals for the DPRK. China stepped up engagement with the DPRK, rather than isolating it. As discussed above, PRC Defense Minister Liang Guanglie visited Pyongyang in November 2009. In December, China's Minister of Public Security hosted and promised material aid to his North Korean counterpart. China's continued support for the DPRK regime could have induced it to negotiate with a greater sense of security, but bolstering the regime proved counterproductive as it became less willing (if it had been willing) to forego its nuclear program as it developed more capabilities.

China could not charge the United States for lack of engagement with China or with the DPRK. President Obama visited Beijing for a summit in November 2009 and discussed with Hu Jintao the goal of the verifiable elimination of North Korea's nuclear weapons program, including through the resumption of the Six-Party Talks "as soon as possible." The Administration also stepped up signals for a robust bilateral dialogue by sending Special Representative Stephen Bosworth to Pyongyang on December 8, 2009, to seek North Korea's return to the Six-Party

---

[111] Quoted by *Voice of America*, June 24, 2009.

[112] *Dandong Ribao*, July 28, 2009; *Chosun Ilbo*, July 30, 2009; *Yomiuri Shimbun*, October 1, 2009.

[113] Author's consultations with close PRC observer of policymaking in Beijing, October 2009; Jonathan Pollack, "Kim Jong Il's Clenched Fist," *Washington Quarterly*, October 2009. As one indication of attitudes in the PRC, a poll conducted by the Lowry Institute and MacArthur Foundation in August-September 2009 found that 34% of those polled considered the United States as the greatest threat, while just 3% considered North Korea as the greatest threat.

Talks and commitment to implement the Joint Statement of 2005. However, Bosworth said that his visit was exploratory, with no commitment from the DPRK, while he reportedly told the DPRK that future talks would have to cover its uranium enrichment program.[114]

DPRK's Attacks and Uranium Enrichment (March and November 2010)

Even after the PRC protested President Obama's notifications to Congress on January 29, 2010, of arms sales to Taiwan, General Secretary Hu Jintao of the Communist Party of China (CPC) sent CPC Director of International Liaison Wang Jiarui to North Korea on February 8 to meet with Kim Jong Il and seek his return to the Six-Party Talks. However, the DPRK's media did not mention a discussion on the Six-Party Talks. Meanwhile, another challenge to re-starting the "Six-Party Talks" to negotiate with North Korea came after it attacked South Korea's naval ship, *Cheonan*, on March 26, 2010, killing 46 sailors. As of late April, Secretary of State Clinton and PRC State Councilor Dai Bingguo still discussed getting North Korea back to the "Six-Party process." However, when Kim Jong Il visited the PRC on May 3-7 and discussed the Six-Party Talks, the State Department on May 4 shifted to stress that South Korea's investigation of the *Cheonan*'s sinking should be completed *before* any announcement from Beijing of a return by North Korea to the talks. On May 20, South Korea announced the finding that North Korea sank the *Cheonan*. At the G-20 summit in Toronto on June 27, 2010, President Obama criticized China for "willful blindness" toward North Korea. Nonetheless, taking a different stance from the United States, South Korea, and other countries, China refused to condemn directly North Korea, including in negotiations for a UNSC Presidential Statement issued on July 9. Still, in that statement, the UNSC condemned the "attack." Later, in July, the PRC's military and then followed by the Foreign Ministry (apparently facing the PLA's pressure) expressed "opposition" to U.S.-ROK exercises in the Yellow Sea aimed at deterring North Korea and improving South Korea's defense, even before the United States and South Korea announced on July 20 they will hold a series of exercises. The State Department's Special Advisor Robert Einhorn acknowledged to the press in Tokyo on August 4, 2010, that the Obama Administration discussed with China the need to tightly enforce sanctions under UNSC Resolutions 1718 and 1874 against North Korea, rather than to capitalize on sanctions imposed by other countries.

With its diplomacy on the defensive, the PRC sent Special Representative Wu Dawei to Washington and other capitals in late August and early September to press for resuming the Six-Party Talks, including suggesting a three-step process of U.S.-DPRK talks, informal talks among the six countries, and then the Six-Party Talks. Later in the month, CPC General Secretary Hu Jintao hosted Kim Jong Il, expressed concern about developments only *after* the UNSC's statement on the *Cheonan*, and stressed "peace and stability" on the Korean peninsula ahead of mentioning "denuclearization." Given the DPRK's missile and nuclear tests, and sinking of the *Cheonan*, the Obama Administration shifted to call the talks explicitly the "six-party process," while doubting the credibility of any announcement in Beijing of repeated talks and looking for results in North Korea's implementation of the existing Joint Statement of 2005.

On September 16, 2010, the Senate Armed Services Committee held a hearing with testimony from the Departments of Defense and State about efforts for stability in the Korean peninsula. However, the challenge continued with North Korea's artillery attack against South Korea on November 23. The month before, the DPRK held a military parade for the 65th anniversary of the Workers' Party of Korea that was reviewed by Kim Jong Il as well as his son, Kim Jong Un, who

---

[114] *Washington Post*, December 28, 2009.

was newly installed as a Vice Chairman of the Central Military Commission. The PRC sent Zhou Yongkang, a member of the top Standing Committee of the Politburo of the CPC to stand next to Kim Jong Il at the military parade on October 10. Days later, the PRC Defense Minister, General Liang Guanglie, hosted in Beijing a DPRK military delegation, with a meeting attended by a PLA Major General of the General Staff Department in charge of military training and arms. Later in the same month, the highest-ranking PLA officer, General Guo Boxiong, a Vice Chairman of the Central Military Commission, visited Pyongyang and met with Kim Jong Il, and in a meeting with his DPRK counterpart, Guo was not reported to raise the nuclear problem.

The PRC faced greater pressure and isolation concerning its support for North Korea. In November 2010, reports revealed that the PRC was blocking a report by a U.N. Panel of Experts on the DPRK's supplies to the nuclear programs of Syria, Iran, and Burma.[115] Russian President Dmitry Medvedev, on November 10, expressed "alarm" about North Korea's nuclear ambitions. Siegfried Hecker of Stanford University saw a sophisticated DPRK uranium enrichment facility with 2,000 centrifuges in a visit on November 12.[116] The DPRK's program raised questions about what equipment and financial transfers across the border did the PRC allow and whether the PRC knew of the uranium enrichment efforts. (Later, on February 16, 2011, the DNI testified to the Senate Select Committee on Intelligence that the DPRK's disclosure supported the longstanding U.S. assessment of the DPRK's uranium enrichment, that the claimed construction in less than 20 months of the new uranium enrichment site at Yongbyon was possible only with previous efforts or foreign assistance, and that the DPRK likely had other such sites.) Then, on November 23, the DPRK launched an artillery attack on South Korea's Yeonpyeong Island, killing four people. On the same day, a PRC delegation went to Pyongyang and signed an economic agreement. Also on the same day, U.S. envoy Stephen Bosworth was in Beijing, and he condemned the DPRK's aggression and called the DPRK's uranium enrichment a violation of UNSC resolutions. The PRC side did not. China responded to the DPRK's provocations by again calling for "consultations" under the Six-Party Talks. While rejecting the Six-Party Talks as a substitute for changes in North Korea's behavior, the State Department shifted from calling for North Korea to comply with international obligations to calling also for China to heed its own obligations.

U.S.-PRC Summit (January 2011) and Later Dialogues

After that DPRK attack and in preparing for PRC leader Hu Jintao's state visit in January 2011, the Obama Administration sought to stabilize the relationship with the PRC and stepped up pressure for it to restrain North Korea and influence its decisions for denuclearization. In December 2010, PLA Air Force General Ma Xiaotian, a Deputy Chief of General Staff, visited Washington for the 11th Defense Consultative Talks (DCT). Under Secretary of Defense for Policy Michele Flournoy and the Chairman of the Joint Chiefs of Staff, Admiral Mike Mullen, pressed the PLA side to help end North Korea's provocations and get it to denuclearize. During his visit to Seoul the same month, Admiral Mullen also publicly criticized China for its "tacit approval" of North Korea. President Obama finally spoke with the PRC's Hu Jintao on December 5, but the White House blamed "scheduling" difficulties for the delayed discussion on North Korea. The PRC was the only country to oppose a UNSC statement on North Korea on December 19, with Russia closer to the U.S. side. Showing that it can influence the DPRK, the PRC called

---

[115] *Reuters*, November 9, 2010; *Daily NK*, Seoul, November 11, 2010.

[116] Siegfried Hecker, "A Return Trip to North Korea's Yongbyon Nuclear Complex," November 20, 2010. Also see David Albright and Paul Brannan, "Satellite Image Shows Building Containing Centrifuges in North Korea," ISIS, November 21, 2010; Siegfried Hecker, "What I Found in North Korea," *Foreign Affairs*, December 9, 2010.

the next day for "maximum restraint," and the DPRK did not fire at the ROK when it held an artillery exercise. The United States also warned North Korea through the U.N. channel.

In January 2011 the PLA belatedly hosted Defense Secretary Robert Gates to provide a positive atmosphere for Hu Jintao's state visit later that month. Gates expressed U.S. appreciation for PRC's help in restraining North Korea but also declared that North Korea, with its programs for nuclear weapons and ICBMs, was becoming a "direct threat" to the United States, a point that President Obama repeated to Hu at the summit. In the **U.S.-PRC Joint Statement** issued at Hu's visit on January 19, 2011, the PRC agreed to express "concern" about the DPRK's uranium enrichment program but stopped short of saying that the program violated the September 2005 Joint Statement and UNSC Resolutions. President Obama unilaterally said that the DPRK's uranium enrichment program was in violation of international obligations. President Obama also stressed to Hu that if China did not restrain North Korea, the United States would have to increase its military presence and military exercises in Northeast Asia.[117] Moreover, at a UNSC meeting on February 23, the PRC blocked adoption and release of a report by the U.N. Panel of Experts on North Korea's uranium enrichment and compliance with U.N. resolutions.[118] Testifying to the Senate Foreign Relations Committee on March 1, Assistant Secretary of State Kurt Campbell stressed cooperation with U.S. allies in Asia before China and Russia. Campbell claimed that China shared the same "goals" of peace and stability, and denuclearization, despite PRC support for the DPRK. He called on China to enhance "effective" implementation of sanctions under UNSC Resolutions 1718 and 1874. In contrast to China's call for Six-Party Talks, Campbell called for a U.N. response to the DPRK's uranium enrichment program. He noted Russia's backing for discussion at the UNSC, confirming China's isolation along with the DPRK.

China stepped up cooperation but remained a concern to the United States and its allies. In April 2011, the PRC proposed another three-step process for resuming ROK-DPRK talks, U.S.-DPRK talks, and Six-Party Talks. However, the United States looked for more than talks to actions by the DPRK that demonstrated better behavior. In May, the State Department called for the release of a report by a U.N. Panel of Experts, reportedly blocked at the UNSC by China, finding that Iran and the DPRK traded illicit missile technology using Air Koryo and Iran Air, including with transshipment through China, and reporting on the DPRK's uranium enrichment program.[119] In May, at a trilateral Japan-ROK-PRC summit in Tokyo, the PRC did not repeat in the declaration its "concern" about the DPRK's uranium enrichment program, contrary to the cited "concern" in the U.S.-PRC Joint Statement in January. The PRC again hosted Kim Jong Il.

Again, the PRC could not deny U.S. efforts at direct dialogue with the DPRK. After the meeting in Pyongyang in December 2009, Special Representative for North Korea Policy Bosworth held another "exploratory meeting" with a "constructive" DPRK delegation at the U.S. Mission to the U.N. in New York on July 28-29, 2011. The United States sought the DPRK's dialogue with the ROK and implementation of obligations under UNSC Resolutions 1718 and 1874 and the Joint Statement of 2005. On August 26, PRC media reported that DPRK ruler Kim Jong Il again visited the PRC and told State Councilor Dai Bingguo that it would resume the Six-Party Talks, but the DPRK's media did not report such a statement. There was another round of U.S.-DPRK talks on October 24-25 in Geneva, but Bosworth reported no breakthrough.

---

[117] *New York Times*, January 20, 2011.

[118] *Reuters*, February 17, 2011; *Telegraph*, February 24, 2011; *Chosun Ilbo*, February 25, 2011.

[119] *Telegraph*, May 12; *Reuters*, May 14; *New York Times*, May 14; *Kyodo*, May 17; *Reuters*, May 18, 2011.

"Leap Day" Agreement and Missile Tests (2012)

The new full-time Special Representative for North Korea Policy, Glyn Davies, visited Beijing in February 2012 for bilateral talks with the DPRK. Afterwards, on February 29, the United States and the DPRK issued "Leap Day" statements about an agreement on the DPRK's missile and nuclear programs and U.S. nutritional aid. However, the statements did not explicitly cover a satellite launch, which was announced for April by the DPRK on March 16. The State Department warned that a launch would violate UNSC Resolutions. The PRC singled out the DPRK for "concern and worry" but did not warn of a violation of UNSC Resolutions. At the Nuclear Security Summit (that included Hu Jintao) in Seoul, President Obama called on March 25 for China to recognize that its long-time approach has not changed the DPRK's behavior. On April 13, the DPRK launched a Taepo Dong-2 intercontinental ballistic missile. However, the launch failed and the first stage fell into the Yellow Sea about 100 miles west of South Korea, according to NORTHCOM. The UNSC issued a Presidential Statement (not resolution) that condemned the DPRK's missile launch as a serious violation of Resolutions 1718 and 1874.

In late November 2012, Xi Jinping, the new General Secretary of the Communist Party of China (CPC), sent CPC Politburo Member Li Jianguo to Pyongyang with a message about Northeast Asian peace and stability but without reported mention of denuclearization. One question has been whether Xi would change China's approach to North Korea. DPRK leader Kim Jong Un met with Li. The next day, however, North Korea announced that it will conduct a "satellite" launch. The PRC Foreign Ministry reacted with a rare reference to restrictions of UNSC resolutions. On December 11, North Korea conducted its first apparently successful test of the three-stage **Taepo Dong-2 long-range missile**, whose first stage fell into the Yellow Sea and second stage fell into the Philippine Sea and which launched an object into orbit. The National Security Council called the test a violation of UNSC Resolutions 1718 and 1874. China called for a "prudent and moderate" response. Considering how to change China's calculus on the situation, an unnamed senior official of the Obama Administration said that U.S. steps (including increased naval patrols in Asia and military exercises with allies) to enhance the region's security in face of North Korea's missile threat "are indistinguishable" from actions that China perceives as part of "containment" aimed at China.[120] Other options would target financial assets, including in China.

Third Nuclear Test (2013)

As North Korea threatened another nuclear test, the PRC Foreign Ministry, on January 14, 2013, shifted to stress "denuclearization" ahead of "stability." Xi Jinping then met on January 23 with an envoy of South Korea's president-elect Park Geun-hye and stressed "denuclearization" on the Korean peninsula. The PRC voted with all other members of the UNSC for **Resolution 2087** to condemn the DPRK's missile test over a month before, and impose travel bans and asset freezes on DPRK entities, including in the PRC. China reportedly tightened customs inspections at Dandong and Dalian for trade with North Korea. Still, North Korea conducted its **third nuclear test** on February 12. The White House called the DPRK's missile and nuclear programs "a threat to U.S. national security." South Korea reported that the test at an underground site detonated a nuclear device with a yield of 6-7 kilotons, more powerful than that in past tests.

Observers questioned whether there would be a critical change in China's calculus about the DPRK, including that its missile and nuclear programs undermine the PRC's goal of "stability."

---

[120] *New York Times*, December 13, 2012.

PRC media editorials, academic articles, and public opinion on the Internet called for toughening up on or abandoning North Korea. Official military news reported on the UNSC's condemnation of the nuclear test and a drill in the Shenyang Military Region that involved a scenario of nuclear, biological, or chemical warfare. The PRC publicly announced monitoring of any nuclear fallout.

Nonetheless, PRC officials expressed opposition to the test and stressed denuclearization but did not condemn the test as a flagrant violation of UNSC resolutions and called for calm and restraint. Beijing continued its balanced approach that includes support for Pyongyang along with incremental implementation of UNSC sanctions. After some U.S.-PRC negotiations, the UNSC voted on March 7 to approve **Resolution 2094**, *inter alia*, to expand the sanctions of 2006 against DPRK entities or individuals, to prevent the provision of financial services or financial transfers if they could contribute to the DPRK's nuclear or missile programs, to call for inspection of cargo, and to define luxury goods (already sanctioned in 2006) for the first time.

Legislation included **H.Res. 65** (Royce), **H.R. 673** (Ros-Lehtinen), and **S. 298** (Menendez). The House Foreign Affairs Committee and Senate Foreign Relations Committee held hearings on March 5 and March 7, 2013. Davies testified that China's full and transparent implementation of sanctions remained critical and that China remained central to altering the DPRK's cost calculus. On March 11, National Security Advisor Tom Donilon said in a speech that no country, including China, should conduct "business as usual" with North Korea as it threatens its neighbors. The Obama Administration took some steps to shape China's calculations as well as deter the DPRK. Defense Secretary Chuck Hagel announced on March 15 the deployments of 14 additional Ground-Based Interceptors (GBIs) at Fort Greely, Alaska, and another TPY-2 radar in Japan; a study for an additional GBI site; and restructuring the SM-3 missile defense program. An unnamed U.S. official stressed a signal to China about the "price to be paid for letting the North Koreans stay on the current path." The PRC took note and responded negatively that stronger missile defenses and military alliances will only intensify antagonism and not solve problems, without mentioning the DPRK. On March 18, Deputy Defense Secretary Ashton Carter said that the Air Force flew B-52 strategic bombers from Guam to South Korea on March 8 and 19 for "routine" exercises, extended deterrence, and a commitment to the alliance with South Korea. (In August, a PLA official, who visited the United States with Defense Minister Chang Wanquan, spoke against pressure and sanctions against North Korea and U.S. military exercises. But in a sign of a debate even in the PLA, a former deputy commander of the Nanjing Military Region wrote in a published article that the DPRK's development of nuclear weapons threatens China.[121])

However, days later, PRC ruler Xi reverted to stressing "stability" before "denuclearization," in a telephone conversation with ROK President Park on March 20. China did not join the PSI. China reportedly enforced UNSC sanctions against certain DPRK entities and banks operating in China or acted against the DPRK's Korea Kwangson Bank sanctioned by the U.S. Department of the Treasury in 2009. China also opposed UNSC sanctions against the DPRK's Foreign Trade Bank, but its account at the Bank of China was closed after the Treasury Department sanctioned the DPRK bank on March 11.[122] Visiting Beijing on May 15, Glyn Davies said that the Bank of China took the "significant step," but not as a PRC government decision. China's response to the DPRK's announcement about re-starting the nuclear reactor at Yongbyon in April was to call for re-starting the Six-Party Talks. China's exports of crude oil to North Korea in January-March 2013 increased 6.7% from the previous year's period, and economic links continued to expand

---

[121] *New York Times*, March 15; Foreign Ministry, March 18; *Xinhua*, August 20; *Global Times*, December 16, 2013.

[122] *Reuters*, March 19; *Chosun Ilbo*, March 20; *Asahi*, March 21; *Reuters*, March 26 and May 7, 2013.

(including in trade, investment, railways, roads, power, and parks). The PRC's support for North Korea persisted despite PRC debates, negative public opinion, and the DPRK's actions against China's interests, including the DPRK military's kidnapping of PRC fishermen in May.[123] The DPRK released the fishermen days before Kim Jong Un sent an envoy to meet with Xi on May 24. Xi shifted to stress "denuclearization" before "stability," but Kim's envoy did not mention denuclearization. President Obama asserted to *PBS* on June 17 that his summit with Xi at Sunnylands, CA, showed he was serious about the DPRK's rejection of denuclearization.

Nonetheless, as Davies said in Seoul on September 10, North Korea continued to assert a status with nuclear weapons and did not show a positive attitude about the purpose of the Six-Party Talks, namely, denuclearization. On September 23, the PRC issued a long list of dual-use items for missile and WMD programs banned from export to the DPRK, in order to implement UNSC resolutions. But Xi indicated a more relaxed attitude, telling ROK President Park in Bali on October 7 that the situation on the Korean peninsula "gradually eased." PRC official Wu Dawei visited Washington later in October, but the Administration did not agree to China's call for renewed Six-Party Talks. With concern about the DPRK's continuing nuclear programs, issues include whether to restart the PRC-preferred talks if they are credible and cover uranium enrichment, press the PRC for more pressure against the DPRK, apply more sanctions against the DPRK, and/or cooperate more closely or trilaterally with allies, Japan and South Korea.

Missile Technology Sales to Syria

A Pentagon report in 2001 said that PRC firms, in addition to North Korean and Russian entities, contributed equipment and technology to Syria's liquid fuel missile program.[124] However, while criticizing DPRK and Russian aid to Syria's ballistic missile development, Under Secretary of State John Bolton did not cite PRC help in a speech at the Heritage Foundation on May 6, 2002. The "Section 721 Reports" did not specify PRC aid for Syria's missile program, until the report for 2010 told Congress in February 2011 that PRC entities supplied missile-related items to Syria.

Policy Issues and Options

Issues for Policy

Weapons proliferation by the PRC and/or its organizations raises policy issues concerning (1) assessments of the nature and seriousness of the PRC government's role in the proliferation threat; (2) the priority of this issue relative to other U.S. interests (i.e., other security issues, Taiwan, trade, human rights); and (3) U.S. leadership and leverage (including the use of sanctions and diplomacy, and congressional actions) to obtain China's cooperation in nonproliferation.

---

[123] *Yonhap*, April 24; *Global Times*, May 20; *Wall Street Journal*, June 6; *Yonhap*, October 7, November 5, 2013; *Reuters*, November 23, 2013.

[124] Secretary of Defense, *Proliferation: Threat and Response*, January 2001.

Debate

Successive Administrations have pursued a policy of "engagement" with Beijing. Some policymakers and advocates stress a cooperative approach. In 1998, President Clinton issued certifications to implement the 1985 Nuclear Cooperation Agreement. The Clinton Administration also encouraged the PRC to join the MTCR and proposed to allow more PRC satellite launches. In November 2000, the State Department agreed to waive sanctions and consider new satellite exports in return for another missile non-proliferation pledge from China. Some officials and experts cite PRC nonproliferation statements as signs that the United States made progress in nonproliferation goals. Some also say that U.S. sanctions are counterproductive and are too broad. Rather, they assert that China needs to recognize nonproliferation for its own national interests and develop stronger export controls, perhaps with U.S. assistance. Also, some stress that China would be more cooperative if brought in to draw up "the rules." Some argue that "entities" in China largely operate without the PRC government's knowledge.

Critics argue that the "engagement" policy needs a tougher approach to counter China's activities that undermine U.S. security interests. They note that PRC weapons proliferation activities have continued and repeated PRC assurances have proved to be unreliable. Also, they say that U.S. security interests are better served with a stronger approach to stigmatize sensitive transfers, which would include some sanctions. Some argue that the United States should not subsidize China's missile and nuclear industries. These proponents tend to see U.S. leverage over China as stronger than China's influence against the United States. Some are skeptical that China sees nonproliferation as in its national interest, since Beijing has made progress in nonproliferation commitments as part of improving relations with Washington (surrounding summits) and tried to use its sales as a form of leverage against Washington, especially on the issue of U.S. arms sales to Taiwan. They stress that PRC export controls are weak, even as government repression can be harsh (e.g., against journalists or dissidents). They also doubt that trade in sensitive nuclear weapons and missile technology can continue without the knowledge of the PRC government and/or its military, especially given the status of certain state-owned and defense-industrial enterprises as "serial proliferators."

The PRC Government's Role

Concerning the debate about any knowledge or approval of the PRC government, at a hearing of the Senate Armed Services Committee on March 19, 2002, DCI George Tenet told Senator Carl Levin that while PRC firms sometimes operate on their own, there are instances in which "activities are condoned by the government." The DCI's January 2003 Section 721 Report to Congress noted that PRC entities could have continued contacts with Pakistani nuclear weapons facilities "without Beijing's knowledge or permission," but this comment was dropped from the April 2003 report. The Director of the Defense Intelligence Agency (DIA), Vice Admiral Lowell Jacoby, testified to the Senate Intelligence Committee on February 24, 2004, that PRC entities "remain involved with nuclear and missile programs in Pakistan and Iran," while "in some cases," the entities were involved without the government's knowledge, implying that there were cases in which the PRC knew of the relationships. The Bush Administration repeatedly waived missile proliferation sanctions on certain activities of the PRC government (vs. "entities"). Reportedly, the State Department communicated to China numerous concerns about proliferation activities in Iran, Syria, North Korea, and Pakistan for many years, including in cables in 2003-2009.[125]

No matter what options are pursued, many argue that U.S. leadership and a forward-looking and credible strategy are needed for dealing with China's rising influence in world affairs. A strategic approach might underpin short-term responses to violations and use both positive and negative sources of leverage. Policy issues often center on summitry, sanctions, and satellite exports.

Foreign and Defense Policies

Summits

After the downturn in U.S.-PRC relations because of the 1989 Tiananmen crackdown, the Clinton Administration resumed high-level exchanges in 1993 and argued that "comprehensive engagement" with China advances U.S. security goals, including nonproliferation. President Clinton granted Jiang Zemin summits in Washington, on October 29, 1997, and in Beijing, on June 29, 1998. Leading up to the 1997 summit, the Administration urged China to adopt "comprehensive, nationwide regulations on nuclear export control." China responded by implementing a set of regulations on nuclear export controls signed by Premier Li Peng on September 10, 1997. The regulations permit nuclear exports to only facilities under IAEA safeguards. China also joined the Zangger Committee (on nuclear trade) on October 16, 1997. Then, China issued new export control regulations on dual-use nuclear items on June 17, 1998. The 1998 summit in Beijing produced an agreement on non-targeting nuclear weapons, and joint statements on South Asia and on biological weapons. But China refused to join the MTCR, saying that it was "actively studying" whether to join.

President Bush raised the unresolved missile proliferation issue in Shanghai in October 2001 and in Beijing in February 2002. As Deputy Secretary of State Richard Armitage arrived in Beijing to discuss the Bush-Jiang summit in Crawford, TX, on October 25, 2002, China, on August 25, 2002, published the missile export control regulations promised in November 2000, along with a control list that is modeled on the MTCR. In addition, on October 14, 2002, the PRC issued regulations for export controls over dual-use biological agents. China continued to approach weapon nonproliferation as more a part of the U.S.-PRC relationship than a commitment to international standards. President Bush called China an "ally" in the fight against terrorism.

With the improvement in U.S.-PRC relations, however, some observers said that President Bush did not forcefully press China's leaders on weapons nonproliferation as a priority issue, even while imposing numerous U.S. sanctions.[126] Briefing reporters on President Bush's meeting with PRC President Hu Jintao in France on June 1, 2003, a senior White House official acknowledged

---

[125] "Inside the Ring," *Washington Times*, July 13 and September 7, 2011.

[126] For example, Robert Einhorn, former Assistant Secretary of State for Nonproliferation in the Clinton Administration, criticized the Bush Administration saying that "sanctions are used, but they are usually simply imposed rather than used as a vehicle for trying to leverage better behavior. ... There seems to be no real strategy today to try to promote continued improvement in China's nonproliferation record," ("China and Non-Proliferation," *National Interest*, April 2, 2003). William Kristol, of the Project for the New American Century, in a memo to opinion leaders, dated June 4, 2003, argued that "real progress in U.S.-China relations is unlikely if the president is less than forceful and candid with his Chinese counterpart on issues of importance to the United States." Also see Susan Lawrence, "U.S. Presses China on Arms, Quietly," *Wall Street Journal*, October 30, 2003.

that the two leaders did not discuss U.S. sanctions on NORINCO (which the Administration had just imposed on May 23, 2003, for missile technology transfers to Iran) and that President Hu did not respond to Bush's general concerns about Iran's nuclear weapons program.[127] In Thailand in October 2003, at another meeting between the two presidents, Bush asserted that they had a "very constructive dialogue" on trade, Iraq, counter-terrorism, and North Korea, but he did not mention weapons proliferation as an issue with China, although the Administration had imposed another set of missile proliferation sanctions on NORINCO a month earlier.[128] As discussed above, President Obama also has used summitry but renewed President Clinton's use of joint statements.

Counter-Terrorism Campaign

The terrorist attacks of September 11, 2001, added a compelling U.S. interest in considering U.S. policy on PRC weapons proliferation. With questions about the viability of Pakistan's government after it gave strong support to the anti-terrorism war, the United States could seek intelligence from the PRC about Pakistan's nuclear weapons as well as cooperation in not further adding to instability in South Asia. Also, the Administration could maintain or strengthen its response to the proliferation problem, since PRC entities have reportedly transferred nuclear, missile, and/or chemical weapons technology to sponsors of terrorism. If the Administration lifts sanctions for cooperating countries, options include waiving proliferation sanctions on the PRC.

Missile Defense

On December 11, 2002, President Bush issued his National Strategy to Combat WMD, resting on the three pillars of counter-proliferation, nonproliferation, and response. The first pillar, counter-proliferation, included interdiction, deterrence, and defense (including preemptive measures and missile defenses). Some say that missile defense plays a critical role in the strategy to counter the proliferation threat. Others say the September 2001 attacks increased doubts about the likelihood of terrorists using missiles for weapons delivery. China has opposed U.S. deployment of missile defense systems and related cooperation with Japan or Taiwan and threatened to increase its nuclear missile force. China is concerned that missile defense would spur an arms race, negate its deterrence capabilities, forge closer U.S.-Taiwan military cooperation, and violate the MTCR. During Defense Secretary William Cohen's visit to China in July 2000, the PRC reportedly warned that it would continue missile proliferation activities if the United States provides missile defense to Taiwan (*Washington Post*, July 12, 2000). Also, top PRC arms control official Sha Zukang warned that the PRC would withhold cooperation on arms control and weapons nonproliferation in response to U.S. deployment of NMD, reported the *Washington Post* (July 14, 2000). Others say that PRC proliferation activities and missile buildups continued regardless.

Proliferation Security Initiative (PSI) and 9/11 Commission

On May 31, 2003, in Poland, President Bush announced the Proliferation Security Initiative (PSI) to step up multinational efforts at interdiction and intelligence-sharing. The United States faces a challenge in obtaining China's cooperation in counter-proliferation (e.g., interdiction of shipments, inspections, or intelligence-sharing), given its long-lasting negative and emotional

---

[127] White House, "Background Press Briefing by Senior Administration Official on the President's Meeting with Chinese President Hu," Evian, France, June 1, 2003.

[128] White House, "Remarks by President Bush and President Hu Jintao of China," Bangkok, October 19, 2003.

reaction to U.S. inspection in 1993 of the PRC ship, *Yinhe*, which was suspected of carrying chemicals for Iran. Also, China could doubt further the credibility of U.S. intelligence after President Bush launched the controversial war in Iraq in 2003 and failed to find WMD there.

China has not joined the PSI. China did not join the 11 original PSI members plus Norway, Denmark, Singapore, and Canada in sending representatives to a meeting in Washington on December 16-17, 2003, even though it took place just days after Premier Wen Jiabao's visit to Washington.[129] In October 2004, a PRC Foreign Ministry spokesman expressed concerns that the PSI might allow "military interception, which is beyond the limits of international law."[130] Nonetheless, Under Secretary of State for Arms Control and International Security John Bolton visited Beijing on February 16, 2004, and he revealed that "in the past several years, we have had cooperation with China in some interdiction efforts." While in Tokyo on October 27, 2004, Bolton said that "we are pleased with China's cooperation with the United States to block the export of chemicals that could have been used in North Korea's nuclear weapons programs."

The 9/11 Commission issued its final report on July 22, 2004, and it urged that the United States encourage China (and Russia) to join the PSI. The 110th Congress considered H.R. 1, the Implementing Recommendations of the 9/11 Commission Act of 2007. The House-passed bill of January 9, 2007, noted that the Commission called on China to participate in PSI. The Senate passed its bill on July 9 without such language. The Conference Report of July 25 adopted the House provisions on the commission's recommendations and on the sense of Congress that the President should expand and strengthen the PSI. The bill became P.L. 110-53 on August 3, 2007.

Export Control Assistance

The United States could assist China to strengthen export controls, including the areas of regulations, licensing, customs, border security, and law-enforcement. The Departments of Commerce and State testified to the Senate Governmental Affairs Subcommittee on International Security, Proliferation, and Federal Services on June 6, 2002, that such exchanges were limited.

Linkage to the Taiwan Question

Periodically, China has tried to link the issues of missile proliferation and U.S. conventional arms sales for Taiwan's self-defense. Congress has exercised oversight of the Administration's response to any direct or indirect linkage. After President George H. W. Bush approved the sale of 150 F-16A/B fighters to Taiwan in September 1992, the PRC ended its participation in the "Arms Control in the Middle East" talks. Moreover, as discussed above, in November 1992, the PRC delivered 34 M-11 missiles to Pakistan, although that transfer took place probably with prior planning and regardless of President Bush's announcement. During the 1998 summit in Beijing, the Clinton White House reportedly considered a PRC request for a U.S. pledge to deny missile defense sales to Taiwan, if China promised to stop missile sales to Iran; but no agreement was reached, reported the *Far Eastern Economic Review* (July 16, 1998). On February 26, 2002, before the Director General in charge of arms control at the PRC Foreign Ministry, Liu Jieyi, attended meetings in Washington on March 4-6, an unnamed PRC Foreign Ministry official told

---

[129] Department of State, "Proliferation Security Initiative: Next Experts Meeting, China's Role," December 3, 2003.

[130] "Ministry of Foreign Affairs Says China Will Not Participate in Proliferation Security Initiative," *Zhongguo Xinwen She*, October 26, 2004.

the *Associated Press* that the United States "can't just accuse us of violating our commitments and at the same time, sell large amounts of arms to Taiwan," since such arms sales are "also a kind of proliferation." On July 24, 2004, *Wen Wei Po*, a PRC-owned newspaper in Hong Kong, quoted an unnamed official of the Foreign Ministry as linking weapons nonproliferation to U.S. arms sales to Taiwan. Nonetheless, State Department officials said that China did not pose Taiwan as a "tactical issue" in discussions about North Korea. (See discussion on North Korea above.) Thus, for many years, the United States has faced challenges in getting China's responsible cooperation in international nonproliferation problems while continuing U.S. policy toward Taiwan, as governed by U.S. interests and the Taiwan Relations Act (TRA) of 1979, P.L. 96-8. (See CRS Report RL30957, *Taiwan: Major U.S. Arms Sales Since 1990*, by Shirley A. Kan.)

Economic Controls

Satellite Exports

There have been debates about using satellite exports to gain China's cooperation in missile nonproliferation. Since 1988, the policy of granting licenses to export satellites and presidential waivers of post-Tiananmen sanctions (Section 902 of P.L. 101-246) have allowed satellites to be exported for launch by China Great Wall Industry Corporation (the same company sanctioned for missile proliferation) and—increasingly—for China's own use. In the Clinton Administration, the National Security Council, in a purported Secret memo on talks leading up to the 1998 U.S.-PRC summit (dated March 12 and printed in the March 23, 1998, *Washington Times*), proposed to expand space cooperation, increase the number of satellite launches, issue a blanket presidential waiver of sanctions, and support China's membership in the MTCR—in return for PRC missile export controls. On November 21, 2000, the State Department said it would waive sanctions, again process—not necessarily approve—licenses (suspended in February 2000) to export satellites to China, and discuss an extension of the bilateral space launch agreement (which later expired at the end of 2001), in return for another PRC promise on missile nonproliferation.

However, on September 1, 2001, the Bush Administration imposed sanctions for two years on the China Metallurgical Equipment Corporation (CMEC), for proliferation of missile technology to Pakistan, denying satellite exports to China. Before those sanctions expired, the State Department determined on August 29, 2003, that NORINCO substantially contributed to missile proliferation of Category II MTCR items and imposed sanctions that again effectively banned satellite exports to China. (See Sanctions below.) The last presidential waiver for satellite exports to China was issued in 1998. (See CRS Report 98-485, *China: Possible Missile Technology Transfers Under U.S. Satellite Export Policy—Actions and Chronology*, by Shirley A. Kan.)

In 2009, Congress passed the FY2010 National Defense Authorization Act (NDAA) (enacted on October 28, 2009, as P.L. 111-84) with Section 1248 to require a report from the Secretaries of Defense and State that assessed the risks of removing the control of satellite exports from the U.S. Munitions List (USML) of the State Department, not later than 180 days after enactment. The Obama Administration submitted an interim "Section 1248 Report" on May 6, 2011, and did not issue the final "**Section 1248 Report**" until April 18, 2012. The report discussed reform of the space export control policy and found that some satellites and components can be moved from the USML to the Commerce Control List (CCL) without harm to national security. Nonetheless, the departments recommended that the CCL support nonproliferation policy and prohibit licenses for the transfer of dual-use satellites and related technology destined for launches by the PRC until it controls missile proliferation activities as it had committed. Congress passed the NDAA for

FY2013 (**P.L. 112-239**) with Section 1261 to remove satellites and related items from the USML, by repealing a section in the FY1999 NDAA (P.L. 105-261). However, Congress continued to prohibit the transfer of satellites to the PRC (and the DPRK and any state sponsor of terrorism).

Sanctions and the "Helms Amendment"

Policy debates concerning PRC technology transfers have often centered on the questions of whether to impose unilateral sanctions under U.S. laws, to enact new legislation to tighten mandates for sanctions or reports, or to integrate the multiple laws. Also, there have been the issues of whether to target the PRC government or PRC "entities" (usually state-owned defense industrial organizations, like **CPMIEC** or **NORINCO**) and whether the PRC government lacks the will or the capability to enforce its stated nonproliferation policy. Decisions on sanctions impact U.S. credibility and leverage on the non-proliferation issue. While certain PRC transfers might not violate any international treaties, sanctions could be required under laws that Congress passed to set U.S. nonproliferation policy and shore up nonproliferation treaties and standards. These laws, as amended, include

- Export-Import Bank Act (P.L. 79-173)

- Arms Export Control Act (AECA) (P.L. 90-629)

- Export Administration Act (EAA) (P.L. 96-72)

- Nuclear Proliferation Prevention Act (Title VIII of P.L. 103-236)

- Iran-Iraq Arms Nonproliferation Act (P.L. 102-484)

- Iran Nonproliferation Act (P.L. 106-178); that became the Iran, North Korea, and Syria Nonproliferation Act (P.L. 109-353)

- Executive Order 12938, as amended by Executive Order 13094

- Executive Order 13382

- Iran Sanctions Act of 1996 (P.L. 104-172); expanded by the Comprehensive Iran Sanctions, Accountability, and Divestment Act of 2010 (P.L. 111-195).

Underlying the question of whether sanctions should be used are disagreements about the most effective approach for curbing dangerous PRC sales and promoting U.S. interests and leadership. Some argue that a cooperative approach, rather than sanctions, is more effective. Others say that current sanctions are not effective in countering the PRC's proliferation practices (especially with certain entities being repeatedly sanctioned, negligible penalties, and sanctions targeting companies but not the government) and that legislation requiring sanctions should be toughened. Still others say sanctions stigmatize countries, signal U.S. resolve, and shore up U.S. credibility on this important security problem. Another approach is to use senior-level diplomacy to achieve goals along with sanctions to deter proliferation. In any case, by 2006, China's government and state-owned defense industrial corporations under U.S. sanctions started to seek U.S. training to strengthen export controls and nonproliferation practices. (See discussion below on training and Internal Compliance Programs (**ICPs**).) This evolution showed that U.S. sanctions worked, with negative impacts on the business of sanctioned entities. Still, any real improvement in policies and practices in response to sanctions could be a basis for lifting sanctions.

As for whether to impose or waive missile proliferation sanctions, on November 21, 2000, the Clinton Administration agreed to waive missile proliferation sanctions, again process—not necessarily approve—licenses to export satellites to China, and discuss an extension of the bilateral space launch agreement, in return for a new PRC pledge on missile nonproliferation and a promise to issue missile export controls. However, continued PRC transfers raised the issue of imposing sanctions. By July 2001, the United States protested to China about its non-compliance with the agreement, reported the *Washington Post* (July 27, 2001). Visiting Beijing ahead of President Bush's trip to Shanghai in October 2001, Secretary of State Powell, on July 28, 2001, noted "outstanding issues" about China's implementation of its November 2000 commitment.

In contrast to the Clinton Administration, the Bush Administration repeatedly imposed sanctions on PRC "entities" (but not the PRC government) for transfers (related to ballistic missiles, chemical weapons, and cruise missiles) to Pakistan and Iran, under the Arms Export Control Act, Export Administration Act, Iran Nonproliferation Act of 2000, Iran-Iraq Arms Nonproliferation Act of 1992, Executive Order 12938, and Executive Order 13382. (See **Table 1**: *PRC Entities Sanctioned for Weapons Proliferation*.) About half of the PRC entities, "serial proliferators," have faced repeated sanctions, raising questions about effectiveness.

Among the actions, on September 1, 2001, the Bush Administration imposed sanctions (for two years) on a PRC company, the China Metallurgical Equipment Corporation (**CMEC**), for proliferation of missile technology (Category II items) to Pakistan. The sanctions had the effect of denying licenses for two years for the export of satellites to China for its use or launch by its aerospace entities, because the Category II sanctions deny U.S. licenses to transfer missile equipment or technology (MTCR Annex items) to any PRC "person," which is defined by the so-called "Helms Amendment" (Section 74(a)(8)(B) of the AECA, P.L. 90-629) as all PRC government activity affecting the development or production of missiles, electronics, space systems, and military aircraft, and the State Department considers that satellites are covered by the MTCR Annex (since it includes satellite parts).

In Beijing with the President in February 2002, National Security Advisor Condoleezza Rice said that the PRC should stop "grandfathering" contracts signed before November 2000. On August 25, 2002, the PRC published missile export control regulations (promised in November 2000), just before Deputy Secretary of State Richard Armitage arrived in Beijing to discuss an upcoming summit, showing that China still viewed nonproliferation in the context of ties with the United States. Armitage welcomed the new regulations but added that further discussions were needed. The State Department stressed that questions remained about enforcement of the controls and reductions in PRC proliferation practices. With questions about enforcement and effectiveness of the controls, President Bush did not waive the sanctions imposed in September 2001.

Moreover, the regulations raised a number of questions, including the roles of the Ministry of Foreign Trade and Economic Cooperation (MOFTEC) and Ministry of Foreign Affairs. Part 1 of that control list (missiles and other delivery systems) and dual-use items (in Part 2) for military use are subject to the Regulations on Administering Arms Exports issued in 1997, under the jurisdiction of the State Council and Central Military Commission. Also, unlike the MTCR, the PRC's regulations on missile-related exports do not state a strong presumption to deny transfers of Category I items or any missiles or other items judged to be intended to deliver any WMD.

In the 107th Congress, Senator Fred Thompson inserted a section in the FY2003 NDAA (enacted as Section 1209 in P.L. 107-314) to require the DCI to submit semi-annual reports that identify PRC and other foreign entities contributing to weapons proliferation. However, in his signing statement, President Bush stated that he would construe this and several other sections in a manner consistent with the President's constitutional authority to "withhold information," if disclosure could harm foreign relations, national security, or the Executive Branch's duties.

Before the September 2001 sanctions expired, the State Department determined on August 29, 2003, that **NORINCO** substantially contributed to missile proliferation of Category II MTCR items in a publicly unidentified country and imposed sanctions for two years that banned the issuance to NORINCO of export licenses or U.S. government contracts for missile equipment or technology, and that banned the importation of NORINCO's products. Complicating U.S. considerations, the "Helms Amendment" again applied—denying exports of satellites to China. But the Bush Administration contended that it was "essential to national security" to waive for one year the sanction on imports when applied to other PRC government activities relating to missiles, electronics, space systems, and military aircraft. The sanctions took effect on September 19, 2003. Within a year, the Administration had to decide on the broader sanctions on imports of non-NORINCO products, which could have affected an estimated $12 billion in imports from the PRC, according to one estimate.[131] After the one-year waiver passed, the State Department, for five times, extended the waiver on the import sanction against certain activities of the PRC government for six more months and permanently waived the sanction in March 2007. However, the Bush Administration did not point to any new nonproliferation cooperation from China.

Still, by 2006, after more U.S. sanctions, China's government and defense-industrial corporations started to seek U.S. training (e.g., from the University of Georgia) to improve export controls and nonproliferation practices. Sanctioned entities such as NORINCO, CMEC, and CGWIC set up **Internal Compliance Programs (ICP)**, working with the Ministries of Foreign Affairs and Commerce. In December 2008, NORINCO and CMEC's presidents signed their companies' statements on adherence to weapons nonproliferation, export control, and internal compliance. However, in July 2011, NORINCO, CPMIEC, and China Xinxing Import and Export Company tried to sell arms worth $200 million to Libya's Muammar al Qadhafi, despite UNSC sanctions.[132]

Options for Congress include maintaining, deleting, or amending the "Helms Amendment," such as changing the language that broadly covers "electronics" or a review by the Commerce Department on whether to change China's "non-market economy" status, based upon which the "Helms Amendment" has broadened missile proliferation sanctions. Another question for congressional oversight concerned whether the Executive Branch enforced sanctions that already were imposed, particularly import bans. In late 2009 and early 2010, the Wisconsin Project on Nuclear Arms Control and the *Wall Street Journal* reported that sanctioned PRC entities, including sub-units of CPMIEC and LIMMT Economic and Trade Co., exported products to U.S. firms or through U.S. ports to other countries after 2006.[133] Afterwards, the Treasury Department's Office of Foreign Assets Control named for sanctions the CPMIEC Shanghai Pudong Company (aka China JMM Import and Export Shanghai Pudong Corporation).

Capital Markets

In the 106th Congress, in May 2000, Senator Fred Thompson introduced S. 2645, the "China Nonproliferation Act," to require annual reviews (based on "credible information"), sanctions,

---

[131] Author's interview with the State Department, November 2003; *Far Eastern Economic Review*, November 6, 2003.

[132] *Globe and Mail*, September 2; *Los Angeles Times*, September 5; *New York Times*, September 12, 2011.

[133] Matthew Godsey, "Chinese Companies Evade U.S. Trade Ban," Wisconsin Project on Nuclear Arms Control, December 15, 2009; Peter Fritsch, "Chinese Evade U.S. Sanctions on Iran," *Wall Street Journal*, January 4, 2010.

and use of the U.S. securities market as a policy tool. In September 2000, the Senate passed (65-32) a motion to table the legislation as an amendment to the bill granting China permanent normal trade relations (PNTR) status. In the 107th Congress, Senator Thompson inserted a section in the FY2003 Intelligence Authorization Act (enacted on November 27, 2002, as Section 827 in P.L. 107-306) to require the DCI to submit annual reports on PRC and other foreign companies that are involved in weapons proliferation and raise funds in U.S. capital markets. Reporting the bill on May 13, 2002, the Senate Intelligence Committee (in S.Rept. 107-149) added that it did not intend to restrict access to those markets. The 108th Congress passed the FY2004 Intelligence Authorization Act (P.L. 108-177) that included Section 361(e) to repeal the reporting requirement.

Nuclear Cooperation and U.S. Export of Reactors

After the PRC promised not to start new nuclear cooperation with Iran on the eve of the 1997 U.S.-China summit, President Clinton, on January 12, 1998, signed certifications (as required by P.L. 99-183) on China's nuclear nonproliferation policy and practices to implement the 1985 Nuclear Cooperation Agreement. According to President Clinton, the agreement would serve U.S. national security, environmental, and economic interests, and "the United States and China share a strong interest in stopping the spread of weapons of mass destruction and other sophisticated weaponry in unstable regions and rogue states—notably, Iran." The President also waived a sanction imposed after the Tiananmen crackdown (in P.L. 101-246). Later, at the 1998 summit, the Department of Energy (DOE) and the PRC State Planning Commission signed an agreement on peaceful nuclear cooperation, including bringing PRC scientists to U.S. national labs, universities, and nuclear facilities.

On February 28, 2005, Westinghouse submitted a bid to sell four AP1000 nuclear power reactors to China, with the NRC's approval. The Bush Administration supported Westinghouse's bid to sell nuclear reactors to China. However, critics said that the United States, including its Export-Import Bank, should not support nuclear exports to China, given proliferation concerns. On June 28, 2005, Representative Bernard Sanders introduced Amendment 381 to the Foreign Operations, Export Financing, and Relations Programs Appropriations Act for FY2006 (H.R. 3057) to prohibit funds from being used by the Export-Import Bank to approve an application for a loan or loan guarantee for a nuclear project in the PRC. The House adopted the amendment (313-114) and passed H.R. 3057 on June 28, 2005, with the language in Section 589. However, this section was dropped in the conference committee (H.Rept. 109-265). While in Beijing on December 16, 2006, Secretary of Energy Samuel Bodman signed a bilateral Memorandum of Understanding that granted the deal to Westinghouse. (See CRS Report RL33192, *U.S.-China Nuclear Cooperation Agreement*, coordinated by Shirley A. Kan.)

Policymakers have options that affect nuclear cooperation with China. Indeed, in 1998, Deputy Assistant Secretary of State for Nonproliferation Robert Einhorn testified to Congress that

> We must, therefore, approach implementation of the agreement with a healthy skepticism. President Reagan's advice to trust but verify is clearly warranted here. So we will be monitoring China's behavior carefully, and the Chinese will know that any actions inconsistent with their commitments will jeopardize future cooperation.[134]

---

[134] House International Relations Committee, hearing, "Implementation of the U.S.-China Nuclear Cooperation Agreement," February 4, 1998.

U.S. Import Controls

While sanctions may affect U.S. exports, some options may affect imports of products produced by PRC military or defense-industrial entities suspected of contributing to proliferation. Import controls have been included as possible sanctions for missile proliferation under Section 73(a)(2)(C) of the AECA and Section 11B(b)(1)(B)(iii) of the EAA, as well as affected by what is popularly called the "Helms Amendment," giving a broad definition of "person" as a target of sanctions. Issues include whether to sanction imports and what the parameters should be.

U.S. Export Controls

Export controls are a policy tool, because U.S. technology provides one source of leverage with respect to Beijing. After the Cold War, U.S. export restrictions have been re-focused to the threat of WMD and missiles. Some in Congress are concerned about U.S. technology reaching hostile states with WMD programs through China. U.S. arms sales to China have been banned under sanctions imposed after the 1989 Tiananmen Crackdown (in P.L. 101-246). However, there are competing economic interests in exporting dual-use technology.

Nonproliferation and Arms Control

Nonproliferation Regimes (MTCR, NSG, etc.)

Another policy approach is to strengthen the international nonproliferation regimes. There are two prongs in such efforts: (1) encouraging PRC support for strengthening the regimes (e.g., the IAEA's verification authority) to enforce compliance and (2) filling gaps in China's participation. Some say that efforts to include China would capitalize on its desire to be treated as a "great power" and to be perceived as a responsible world leader. In addition, they stress that China would be more cooperative if it helped to draw up the "rules." Others argue that China's participation would risk its obstruction of tighter export controls, possible derailing of arms control efforts, linkage of nonproliferation issues to the Taiwan issue, and access to intelligence-sharing. One basis for this view is the experience with the Arms Control in the Middle East effort in the early 1990s, in which China refused to cover missiles in the effort and later suspended its participation after President George H. W. Bush decided in 1992 to sell Taiwan F-16 fighters.

Options for U.S. policy have included support or opposition to China joining the MTCR (as a member after it establishes a record of compliance and effective export controls), Nuclear Suppliers Group (NSG), Australia Group (on chemical and biological weapons), Wassenaar Arrangement (military and dual-use export controls), and International Code of Conduct Against Ballistic Missile Proliferation. Previously, President Clinton's National Security Council, in a purported Secret memo, dated March 12, 1998 (printed in the March 23, 1998, *Washington Times*), proposed in a "China missile deal" to expand space cooperation with Beijing, increase the number of satellites that China can launch, issue a blanket presidential waiver of post-Tiananmen sanctions on satellite launches, and support China's membership in the MTCR—in return for effective PRC missile export controls.

Critics say that membership in the MTCR would exempt China from certain sanctions, provide it with intelligence, give it a potentially obstructionist role in decision-making, and relax missile-related export controls to China. In September 1999, Congress passed the FY2000 NDAA (**P.L. 106-65**), stating its sense that the President shall take steps to obtain an agreement with the PRC on adherence to the MTCR and its annex and that the PRC should not be allowed to join the

MTCR without meeting certain conditions. It also required a report on the PRC's adherence to the MTCR. The classified report was submitted on August 18, 2000. In 2004, China applied to join the MTCR but was not accepted as a member, according to the DNI's Section 721 Report to Congress of 2006. Though China is not a member, the MTCR Chair has contacted China.

China joined the Zangger Committee (on nuclear trade) in October 1997, before a summit in Washington. Also, China issued new export control regulations on dual-use nuclear items on June 17, 1998, before another summit in Beijing.

For years, China was the only major nuclear supplier to shun the multinational NSG, which requires "full-scope safeguards" (IAEA inspections of *all* other declared nuclear facilities in addition to the facility importing supplies to prevent diversions to weapon programs). In January 2004, China applied to join the NSG. However, on May 5, 2004, China signed a contract to build a second nuclear power reactor (Chashma-2) in Pakistan. This contract raised questions because of continuing PRC nuclear cooperation with Pakistan and its signing right before a decision by the NSG on China's membership. With a pre-existing contract, Chashma-2 would be exempted from the NSG's requirement for full-scope safeguards.[135] The Bush Administration supported China's membership, after reportedly strident debate between officials who questioned China's commitment to nonproliferation and those who wanted to encourage China's cooperation.[136]

On May 18, 2004, the House International Relations Committee held a hearing to question whether the Administration should support China's membership in the NSG, given concerns about PRC nuclear cooperation with Pakistan and Iran, about whether China would be a spoiler in the NSG, and about loss of U.S. leverage. Assistant Secretary of State John Wolf testified that the United States urged China to join the NSG since 1995, that China was not a spoiler in the Zangger Committee, and that NSG membership would add multilateral influence on China's nuclear technology export policies. Wolf conceded, however, that Pakistan had a nuclear weapons program and did not accept full-scope safeguards, and that the United States preferred that no country provide Pakistan with benefits of peaceful nuclear cooperation. He noted that the Chashma-2 plant will be under IAEA safeguards, but the NSG exempts full-scope safeguards for contracts signed before NSG membership. Wolf also acknowledged that the Administration did not request that Beijing use its influence with Islamabad to secure tighter Pakistani export controls. Moreover, he conceded that the Administration had not seen the contract for Chashma-2 nor received the requested "full information" on any ongoing nuclear cooperation projects that China sought to grandfather. A memo dated May 26, 2004, by the Project for the New American Century criticized the Administration's decision for turning a "blind eye to China's reactor sales to Pakistan." The NSG decided at a meeting on May 28 to accept China as a member. In later years, China has bolstered the concerns about whether it has played a spoiler by providing additional reactors to Pakistan, beyond Chashma-2. The Carnegie Endowment argued in 2011 that China's so-called "grandfathering" of Chashma-3 and -4 reactors further eroded the NSG and warned of damage to the NSG's credibility.[137]

---

[135] "Pakistan, China Agree on Second Chashma Unit," *Nucleonics Week*, May 6, 2004.

[136] Carol Giacomo, "U.S. Backs China Joining Nuclear Group," *Reuters*, May 11, 2004.

[137] Toby Dalton, Mark Hibbs, and George Perkovich, "A Criteria-Based Approach to Nuclear Cooperation with Pakistan," Carnegie Endowment for International Peace, June 22, 2011; Mark Hibbs, "The Future of the Nuclear Suppliers Group," Carnegie Report, December 2011.

CTBT, Fissile Materials, and Nuclear Security

China, on July 30, 1996, began a moratorium on nuclear testing and signed the Comprehensive Test Ban Treaty (CTBT) on September 24, 1996. However, after the U.S. Senate rejected (51-48) the treaty on October 13, 1999, it became doubtful that the PRC would ratify the CTBT. Also, the United States has sought PRC cooperation on negotiating a global ban on the production of fissile materials for nuclear weapons and other nuclear explosive devices. On October 4, 1994, the United States and China agreed to "work together to promote the earliest possible achievement of a multilateral, non-discriminatory, and effective verifiable convention" banning fissile materials production. The PRC could follow if the United States ratified the CTBT. President Obama issued a U.S.-PRC Joint Statement at the Obama-Hu summit in Beijing on November 17, 2009, in which the two countries committed to pursue "ratification" of the CTBT "as soon as possible," to work together for the early entry into force of the CTBT, and to support the launching of negotiations on the Fissile Material Cut-off Treaty. At Hu Jintao's state visit in Washington on January 19, 2011, the U.S.-PRC Joint Statement did not mention ratification in calling again for the early entry into force of the CTBT. The two countries reaffirmed cooperation based on the Nuclear Security Summit in Washington in April 2010 (attended by Hu Jintao) and signed a Memorandum of Understanding to set up a "Center of Excellence on Nuclear Security" in China.

Congress passed the NDAA for FY2011 (P.L. 111-383). Section 1303 limited the use of funds to no more than $500,000 in FY2011 under the Cooperative Threat Reduction program to set up a center of excellence in any country outside of the former Soviet Union until 15 days after the Defense Secretary submitted a report with required information. Also, Section 1304 required the Secretaries of Defense and Energy to submit by April 1, 2011, a plan to Congress concerning activities with the PRC under the Cooperation Threat Reduction Program and Defense Nuclear Nonproliferation Program during FYs 2011 through 2016, including costs paid by the PRC.

The House on May 26, 2011, passed H.R. 1540, the NDAA for FY2012, with Section 3112 to stipulate that not more than $7 million may be obligated or expended for the U.S.-China Center of Excellence on Nuclear Security until the Secretary of Energy reports to Congress on a review of the PRC's capacity to develop and implement training in best practices for nuclear security and on how the center's activities could contribute to improving China's record on proliferation. The Senate Armed Services Committee reported S. 1253 on June 22, without a similar section. Enacted on December 31, 2011, Section 3111 of P.L. 112-81 stipulated that not more than 25% of authorized funds may be used to establish a center of excellence in a country that is not of the former Soviet Union (dropping explicit mention of China) until Congress receives the report.

Intermediate-range Nuclear Forces (INF) Treaty

Under the 1987 Treaty on the Elimination of Intermediate-Range and Shorter-Range Missiles (INF Treaty) with the Soviet Union, the United States eliminated by 1991 all ground-launched ballistic and cruise missiles with ranges between 500 and 5,500 km. By 2010, China had the world's most active land-based ballistic and cruise missile program, including development of the world's only anti-ship ballistic missile (ASBM). Former Pentagon officials proposed in 2011 an option to expand the INF Treaty to include China, as a response to the instability raised by its missile buildup for Taiwan, Asian allies, the United States, and others.[138]

---

[138] Mark Stokes, Dan Blumenthal, "Why China's Missiles Should Be Our Focus," *Washington Post*, January 2, 2011.

Table 1. PRC Entities Sanctioned for Weapons Proliferation

Entity/Person (or successor, sub-unit, subsidiary)	Reason: Statutes	Effective Dates
- China Great Wall Industry Corporation	Missile Proliferation:	June 25, 1991
- China Precision Machinery Import/Export Corp. (CPMIEC)	§73(a)(2)(A), Arms Export Control Act	waived on March 23, 1992
	§11B(b)(1)(B)(i), Export Administration Act	
	(Category II items in MTCR Annex to Pakistan)	
Ministry of Aerospace Industry, including CPMIEC,	Missile Proliferation:	August 24, 1993
and related entities, including:	§73(a)(2)(A), Arms Export Control Act	waived on November 1, 1994
- China National Space Administration	§11B(b)(1)(B)(i), Export Administration Act	
- China Aerospace Corp.	(Category II items in MTCR Annex to Pakistan)	
- Aviation Industries of China		
- CPMIEC		
- China Great Wall Industry Corp. or Group		
- Chinese Academy of Space Technology		
- Beijing Wan Yuan Industry Corp. (aka Wanyuan Company or China Academy of Launch Vehicle Technology)		
- China Haiying Company		
- Shanghai Astronautics Industry Bureau		
- China Chang Feng Group (aka China Changfeng Company)		

Entity/Person (or successor, sub-unit, subsidiary)	Reason: Statutes	Effective Dates
5 PRC citizens:	CW Proliferation:	May 21, 1997
- Liao Minglong	§81(c), Arms Export Control Act	
- Tian Yi	§11C(c), Export Administration Act	
- Chen Qingchang (aka Q.C. Chen)	(dual-use chemical precursors, equipment, and/or technology to Iran)	
- Pan Yongming		
- Shao Xingsheng		
2 PRC companies:		
- Nanjing Chemical Industries Group		
- Jiangsu Yongli Chemical Engineering and Technology Import/Export Corp.		
I Hong Kong company:		
- Cheong Yee Ltd.		
Jiangsu Yongli Chemicals and Technology Import/Export Corp.	CW/BW Proliferation: §3, Iran Nonproliferation Act	June 14, 2001 for two years
China Metallurgical Equipment Corp. (aka CMEC, MECC)	Missile Proliferation: §73(a)(2)(A), Arms Export Control Act §11B(b)(1)(B)(i), Export Administration Act (MTCR Category II items to Pakistan)	September 1, 2001 for two years
- Liyang Chemical Equipment	CW/BW Proliferation: §3, Iran Nonproliferation Act (Australia Group controls)	January 16, 2002 for two years
- China Machinery and Electric Equipment Import/Export Co.		
- Q.C. Chen		

Entity/Person (or successor, sub-unit, subsidiary)	Reason: Statutes	Effective Dates
- Liyang Yunlong (aka Liyang Chemical Equipment Co.) - Zibo Chemical Equipment Plant (Chemet Global Ltd.) - China National Machinery and Electric Equipment Import and Export Co. - Wha Cheong Tai Co. - China Shipbuilding Trading Co. - CPMIEC - China Aero-Technology Import/ Export Corp. (CATIC) - Q.C. Chen	Weapons Proliferation: §3, Iran Nonproliferation Act (AG-controlled items and conventional weapons-related technology related to unspecified missiles)	May 9, 2002 for two years
- Jiangsu Yongli Chemicals and Technology Import Export Corp. - Q.C. Chen - China Machinery and Equipment Import Export Corp. - China National Machinery and Equipment Import Export Corp. - CMEC Machinery and Electric Equipment Import Export Co. - CMEC Machinery and Electrical Import Export Co. - China Machinery and Electric Equipment Import Export Co. - Wha Cheong Tai Co. - China Shipbuilding Trading Co.	Weapons Proliferation: §1604(b), Iran-Iraq Arms Non-Proliferation Act and §81(c), Arms Export Control Act §11C(c), Export Administration Act (chemical weapons technology to Iran) only under Iran-Iraq Arms Nonproliferation Act (cruise missile technology)	July 9, 2002 for two years Sanctions were lifted on June 21, 2013, on China Machinery and Equipment Import Export Corporation, China National Machinery and Equipment Import Export Corporation, CMEC Machinery and Electric Equipment Import and Export Company, CMEC Machinery and Electrical Import Export Company, and China Machinery and Electric Equipment Import and Export Company.
North China Industries Corporation (NORINCO)	Missile Proliferation: Executive Order 12938 (amended by Executive Order 13094) (missile technology to Iran)	May 23, 2003 for two years

Entity/Person (or successor, sub-unit, subsidiary)	Reason: Statutes	Effective Dates
- Taian Foreign Trade General Corporation - Zibo Chemical Equipment Plant - Liyang Yunlong Chemical Equipment Group Company - NORINCO - CPMIEC	Missile Proliferation: §3, Iran Nonproliferation Act	June 26, 2003 for two years
CPMIEC	Missile Proliferation: Executive Order 12938 (as amended by Executive Order 13094) (missile technology to publicly unnamed country)	July 30, 2003 for indefinite period
NORINCO	Missile Proliferation: §73(a)(2)(A) and (C), Arms Export Control Act §11B(b)(1)(B)(i) and (iii), Export Administration Act (Substantial contribution in proliferation of MTCR Category II technology to publicly unnamed country)	September 19, 2003 for two years; waived for one year on import ban for non-NORINCO products; waiver extended on September 18, 2004, for six months; waived for six months on March 18, 2005; waived for six months on September 18, 2005; waived on September 18, 2006; waived on September 18, 2006, for six months; permanently waived on March 18, 2007.
- Beijing Institute of Opto-Electronic Technology (BIOET) - NORINCO - CPMIEC - Oriental Scientific Instruments Corporation (OSIC) - Zibo Chemical Equipment Plant (aka Chemet Global Ltd., South Industries Science and Technology Trading Company)	Weapons Proliferation: §3, Iran Nonproliferation Act (transfers to Iran controlled under multilateral export control lists or having the potential to make a material contribution to WMD or cruise or ballistic missiles)	April 1, 2004 for two years
- Xinshidai (aka China Xinshidai Company, XSD, China New Era Group, or New Era Group)	Missile proliferation: Executive Order 12938 (as amended by Executive Order 13094) (material contribution to missile proliferation in publicly unnamed country)	September 20, 2004 for two years

Entity/Person (or successor, sub-unit, subsidiary)	Reason: Statutes	Effective Dates
- Beijing Institute of Aerodynamics - BIOET - China Great Wall Industry Corporation - NORINCO - LIMMT Economic and Trade Company, Ltd. - OSIC - South Industries Science and Technology Trading Co.	Weapons Proliferation: §3, Iran Nonproliferation Act (transfers to Iran controlled under multilateral export control lists or having the potential to make a material contribution to WMD or cruise or ballistic missiles)	September 23, 2004 for two years
- Liaoning Jiayi Metals and Minerals Co. - Q.C. Chen - Wha Cheong Tai Co. Ltd. - Shanghai Triple International Ltd.	Weapons Proliferation: §3, Iran Nonproliferation Act (transfers to Iran controlled under multilateral export control lists or having the potential to make a material contribution to WMD or cruise or ballistic missiles)	November 24, 2004 for two years
- Beijing Alite Technologies Company Ltd. - CATIC - China Great Wall Industry Corporation - NORINCO - Q.C. Chen - Wha Cheong Tai Company (aka Wah Cheong Tai Co., Hua Chang Tai Co.) - Zibo Chemet Equipment Corp. (aka Chemet Global Ltd)	Weapons Proliferation: §3, Iran Nonproliferation Act (transfers to Iran controlled under multilateral export control lists or having the potential to make a material contribution to WMD or cruise or ballistic missiles)	December 27, 2004 for two years
-CATIC -NORINCO -Hongdu Aviation Industry Group -LIMMT Metallurgy and Minerals Company Ltd. -Ounion (Asia) International Economic and Technical Cooperation Ltd. -Zibo Chemet Equipment Company	Missile and CW Proliferation: §3, Iran Nonproliferation Act (transfers to Iran controlled under multilateral export control lists or having the potential to make a material contribution to WMD or cruise or ballistic missiles)	December 23, 2005 for two years

Entity/Person (or successor, sub-unit, subsidiary)	Reason: Statutes	Effective Dates
-Be jing Alite Technologies Company Ltd. (ALCO) -LIMMT Economic and Trade Company Ltd. -China Great Wall Industry Corporation (CGWIC) -CPMIEC -G.W. Aerospace (a U.S. office of CGWIC)	Missile Proliferation: Executive Order 13382 (transfers to Iran's military and other organizations of missile and dual-use components, including items controlled by the MTCR)	June 13, 2006 On June 19, 2008, sanctions lifted against CGWIC and G.W. Aerospace
Great Wall Airlines (aka Changcheng Hangkong)	Missile Proliferation: Executive Order 13382 (unspecified transfers probably to Iran)	August 15, 2006 lifted on December 12, 2006
-China National Electronic Import-Export Company -CATIC -Zibo Chemet Equipment Company	Weapons Proliferation: §3, Iran, North Korea, and Syria Nonproliferation Act (transfers controlled under multilateral export control lists or having the potential to make a material contribution to WMD or cruise or ballistic missiles)	December 28, 2006 for two years
-CPMIEC -Shanghai Non-Ferrous Metals Pudong Development Trade Company Ltd. -Zibo Chemet Equipment Company	Weapons Proliferation: §3, Iran, North Korea, and Syria Nonproliferation Act (transfers controlled under multilateral export control lists or having the potential to make a material contribution to WMD or cruise or ballistic missiles)	April 17, 2007 for two years
-China Xinshidai Company -China Shipbuilding and Offshore International Corporation -Huazhong CNC	Weapons Proliferation: §3, Iran, North Korea, and Syria Nonproliferation Act (transfers controlled under multilateral export control lists or having the potential to make a material contribution to WMD or cruise or ballistic missiles)	October 23, 2008 for two years
-Dalian Sunny Industries (aka LIMMT Economic and Trade Company, LIMMT (Dalian) Metallurgy and Minerals Company, and LIMMT (Dalian FTZ) Economic and Trade Organization) -Bellamax	Missile Proliferation: §73(a)(1), Arms Export Control Act §11B(b)(1), Export Administration Act	February 2, 2009 for two years Waived for PRC government activities related to missiles, electronics, space systems, and military aircraft

Entity/Person (or successor, sub-unit, subsidiary)	Reason: Statutes	Effective Dates
-Dalian Sunny Industries (aka LIMMT Economic and Trade Company, LIMMT (Dalian) Metallurgy and Minerals Company, and LIMMT (Dalian FTZ) Economic and Trade Organization) -Bellamax	Missile Proliferation: Executive Order 12938	February 2, 2009 for two years
-Fangwei LI (aka Karl LEE), c/o LIMMT Economic and Trade Company	Missile Proliferation: Executive Order 13382	April 7, 2009
-Karl LEE -Dalian Sunny Industries (aka LIMMT (Dalian) Metallurgy and Minerals Co., LIMMT (Dalian) Economic and Trade Organization, Liaoning Industry and Trade Co.) -Shanghai Technical By-Products International (STBPI) -Zibo Chemet Equipment Company	Weapons Proliferation: §3, Iran, North Korea, and Syria Nonproliferation Act (transfers controlled under multilateral export control lists or having the potential to make a material contribution to WMD or cruise or ballistic missiles)	July 14, 2010 for two years
Entities in Hong Kong apparently associated with Iran: -Advance Novel Limited -Alpha Effort Limited -Best Precise Limited -Concept Giant Limited -Great Method Limited -Ideal Success Investments -Logistic Smart Limited -Neuman Limited -New Desire Limited -Partner Century Limited -Sackville Holdings Limited -Sandford Group Limited -Sino Access Holdings Limited -Smart Day Holdings Group -Starry Shine International Limited -System Wise Limited	Weapons Proliferation: Executive Order 13382	January 13, 2011

Entity/Person (or successor, sub-unit, subsidiary)	Reason: Statutes	Effective Dates
-Top Glacier Company Limited		
-Top Prestige Trading Limited		
-Trade Treasure Limited		
-True Honour Holdings Limited		
-Karl LEE	Weapons Proliferation:	May 23, 2011
-Dalian Sunny Industries	§3, Iran, North Korea, and Syria Nonproliferation Act	for two years
-Dalian Zhongbang Chemical Industries Company	(transfers controlled under multilateral export control lists or having the potential to make a material contribution to WMD or cruise or ballistic missiles)	
-Xian Junyun Electronics		
-Xun WANG (PPG Paints Trading Company)	Nuclear Proliferation: §13(c), Export Administration Act (export of paint to Chasma 2 nuclear power plant under control of the Pakistan Atomic Energy Commission)	November 16, 2011
-Dalian Sunny Industries (LIMMT)	Weapons Proliferation:	December 20, 2011
-Karl LEE (LI Fangwei)	§3, Iran, North Korea, and Syria Nonproliferation Act	for two years
-Zibo Chemet Equipment Company	(transfers controlled under multilateral export control lists or having the potential to make a material contribution to WMD or cruise or ballistic missiles)	
-Zhuhai Zhenrong Company	Nuclear Proliferation: Iran Sanctions Act, as amended by CISADA (transfers of gasoline to Iran)	January 12, 2012
-Bank of Kunlun	CISADA (significant financial transactions for Iran's banks)	July 31, 2012
Entities in Beijing and Hong Kong associated with DPRK:	Weapons Proliferation:	January 24, 2013
-KIM Kwang-Il, Tanchon Commercial Bank official	Executive Order 13382	
-RA Kyong-Su, Tanchon Commercial Bank official	(sales of conventional weapons and ballistic missiles)	
-Leader (Hong Kong) International Trading Limited		

Entity/Person (or successor, sub-unit, subsidiary)	Reason: Statutes	Effective Dates
-BST Technology and Trade Company	Weapons Proliferation:	February 5, 2013
-CPMIEC	§3, Iran, North Korea, and Syria Nonproliferation Act	for two years
-Dalian Sunny Industries (aka LIMMT)	(transfers controlled under multilateral export control lists or having the potential to make a material contribution to WMD or cruise or ballistic missiles)	
-Karl LEE (aka LI Fangwei)		
-Poly Technologies		
-Dalian Sunny Industries	Missile Proliferation:	February 11, 2013
-Karl LEE (aka LI Fangwei)	Executive Order 12938	for two years
-Dalian Sunny Industries	Missile Proliferation:	February 11, 2013
-Karl LEE (aka LI Fangwei)	§73(a)(1), Arms Export Control Act	for two years
	§11B(b)(1), Export Administration Act	
Entities in Dalian associated with DPRK:	Weapons Proliferation in or by DPRK:	March 7, 2013
-YO'N Cho'ng-Nam, KOMID official	Executive Order 13382	
-KO Ch'o'l-Chae, KOMID official		
Entity in Dalian associated with DPRK:	Weapons Proliferation in or by DPRK:	June 27, 2013
-KIM Chol Sam, Daedong Credit Bank	Executive Order 13382	

Note: This table summarizes the unclassified discussion of sanctions in this CRS Report and was compiled based on publication of notices in the *Federal Register*, reports and statements of the Administration, legislation enacted by Congress, and news reports.

Author Contact Information

Shirley A. Kan
Specialist in Asian Security Affairs
skan@crs.loc.gov, 7-7606